THE MUSIC TREE
ACTIVITIES

$14.99

PART 2A

by
Frances Clark
Louise Goss
Sam Holland
Steve Betts

Educational Consultants:
Steve Betts, Yat Yee Chong
Linda Christensen, Ted Cooper
Amy Glennon, Monica Hochstedler
Peter Jutras, Elvina Pearce
Mary Frances Reyburn, Craig Sale

ISBN 0-87487-951-5

PREFACE

We are proud to present this latest revision of **THE MUSIC TREE,** the most carefully researched and laboratory-tested series for elementary piano students available. This edition combines the best of the old and the new—a natural, child-oriented sequence of learning experiences that has always been the hallmark of Frances Clark materials, combined with new music of unprecedented variety and appeal. Great pedagogy and great music—a winning combination!

THE MUSIC TREE consists of the eight books listed below, to be used in sequence. Each has a textbook and an activities book to be used together:

TEXTBOOKS	ACTIVITIES BOOKS
TIME TO BEGIN (the primer)	**TIME TO BEGIN ACTIVITIES**
MUSIC TREE 1 (formerly A)	**ACTIVITIES 1**
MUSIC TREE 2A (formerly B)	**ACTIVITIES 2A**
MUSIC TREE 2B (formerly C)	**ACTIVITIES 2B**

Used together, these companion volumes provide a comprehensive plan for musical growth at the piano and prepare for the intermediate materials that follow at Levels 3 and 4.

We are deeply indebted to the students and faculty of The New School for Music Study and the Southern Methodist University Preparatory Department, who have been the inspiration and proving ground for this new edition, and to our educational consultants who have reviewed and tested the materials at every step of their development.

These are among the last materials on which Frances Clark was able to work personally, and it is to her memory that the books are lovingly dedicated.

It is our hope that **THE MUSIC TREE** will provide for you the same success and delight in teaching that we have experienced, and that your students will share with ours the excitement of this new adventure in learning.

CONTENTS

Reading

Naming Notes

Circle the correct music for each group of letter names.

For correlated Discoveries, Repertoire and Technic, see MUSIC TREE 2A, pages 4-9.

Copying

Copy the notes in each measure on the opposite staff.
In each activity, the first example is done to show you how.

Matching

Draw a line to connect the interval on each keyboard and staff to the correct box in the middle column.

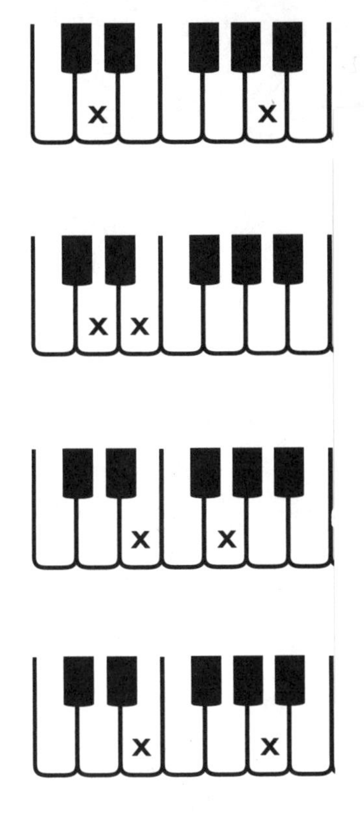

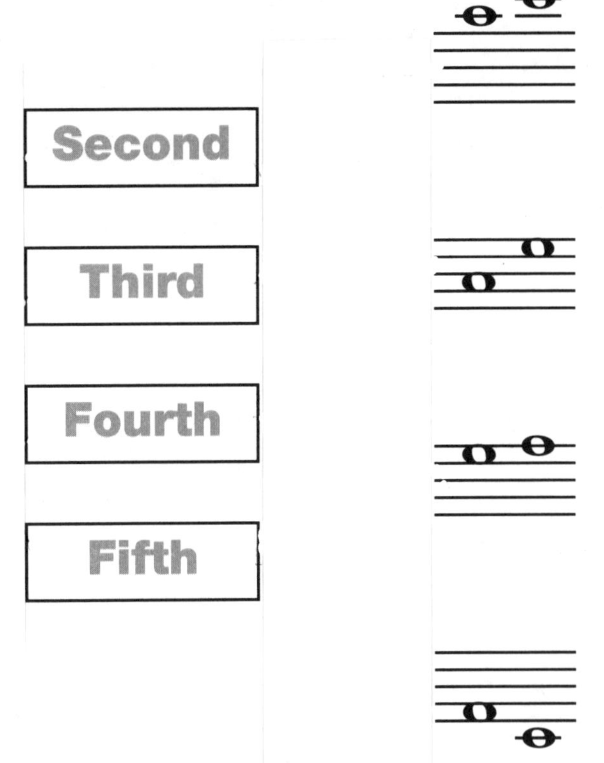

Rhythm

Eighth Notes

1. Swing and say the rhyme with a strong rhythmic pulse, one full arm swing for each pulse.

Yankee Doodle

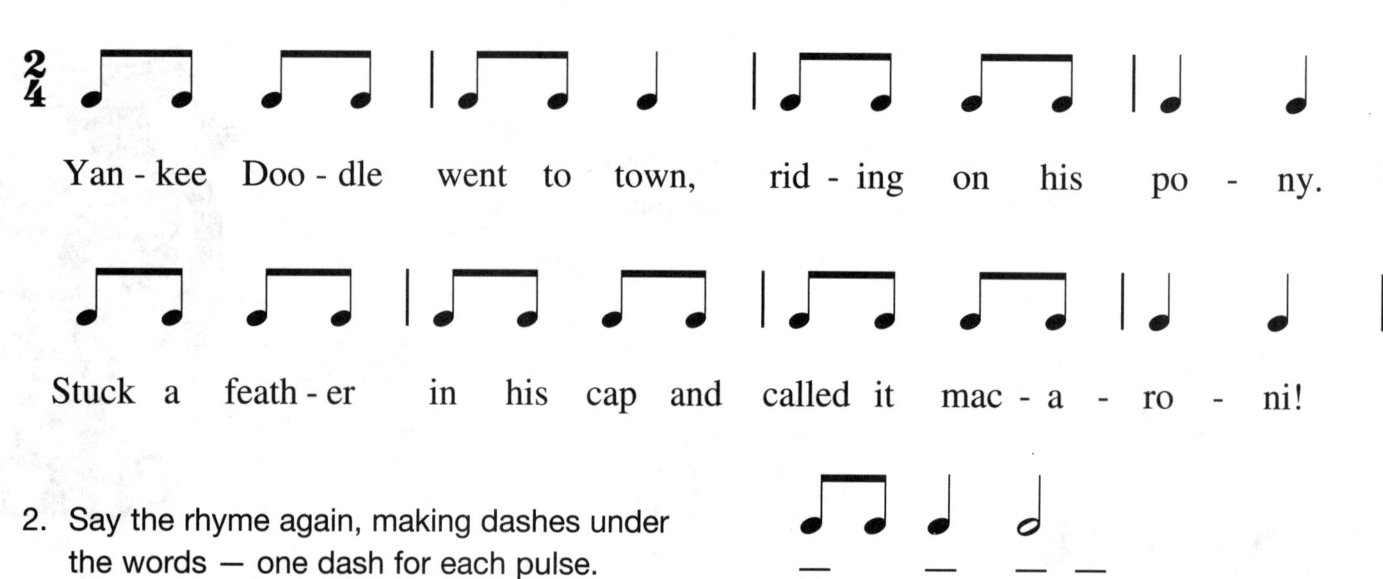

2. Say the rhyme again, making dashes under the words — one dash for each pulse.

3. Then walk the rhythm as you say the rhyme, taking one step for each pulse.

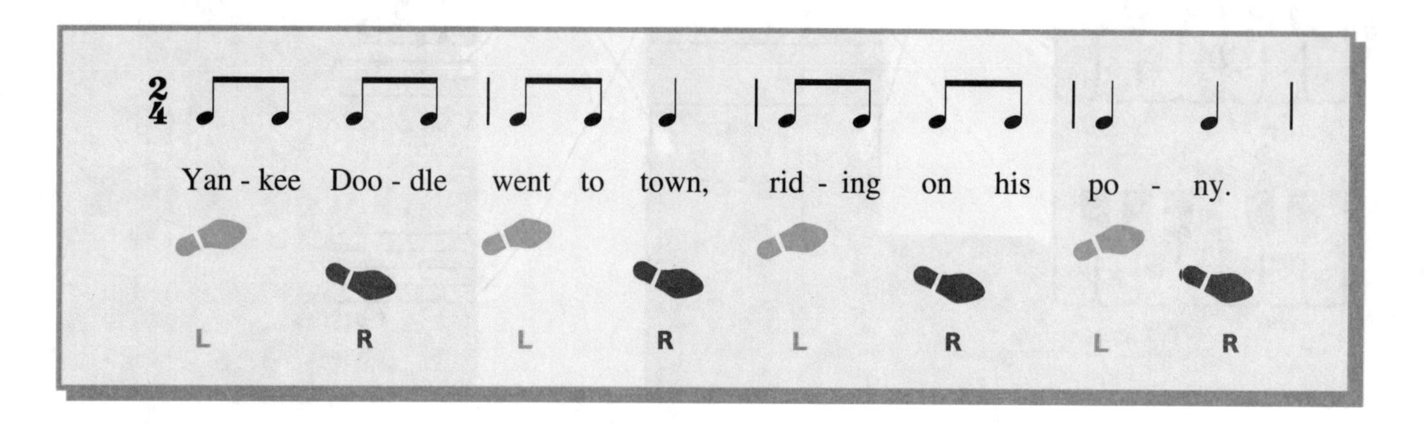

Counting Eighth Notes

In each of these rhythms, set a strong rhythmic pulse:

1. Point and count — point to each note as you count aloud.
2. Tap and count — tap lightly with your fingertips on the keyboard cover or a table — one tap for each note.

Playing Eighth Notes

With each of these eighth-note pieces:

- point and count the rhythm
- tap and count the rhythm
- play and count — RH alone, then LH alone (play each exercise, first using fingers 432, then fingers 321, and finally fingers 543)

Sight-Playing

Sight-playing is playing a piece **at first sight** without practice.
Here are the steps:

1. Circle the clef. Then prepare your hand/s and fingers on the correct keys.
2. Set a **slow** tempo, counting two measures out loud in a strong rhythmic pulse.
3. Play and count with a full tone, **no stopping** from beginning to end.

1.

2.

3.

4.

5.

Word Chain

In this puzzle the last letter of the first word becomes the first letter of the next word. Clues are given below each chain.

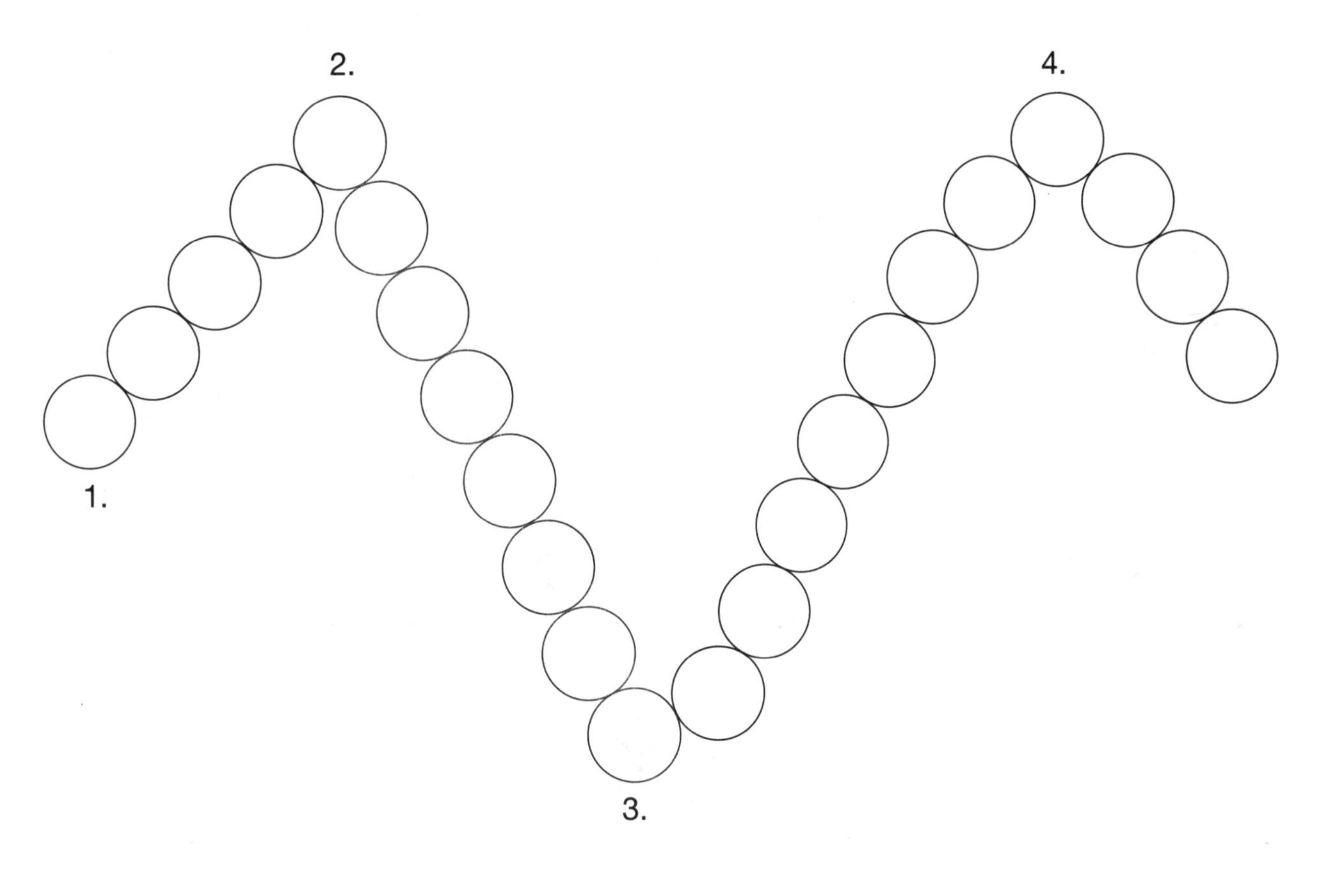

1. 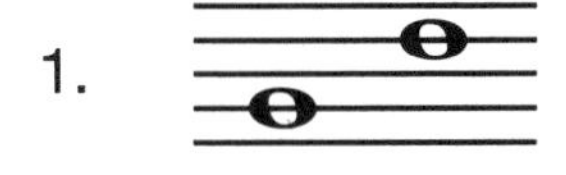

2. ▬

3. 

4. 

Theory

Half Steps

From one key to the very next key is a HALF STEP.
Half steps can look **three** different ways on the keyboard:

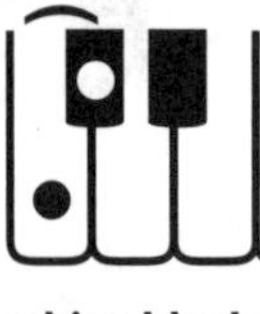

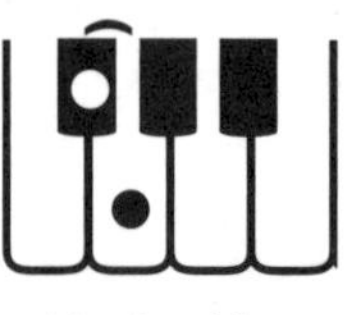

Circle the half steps in this jumble.

Mark an X on the key a half step **above** each dotted key.

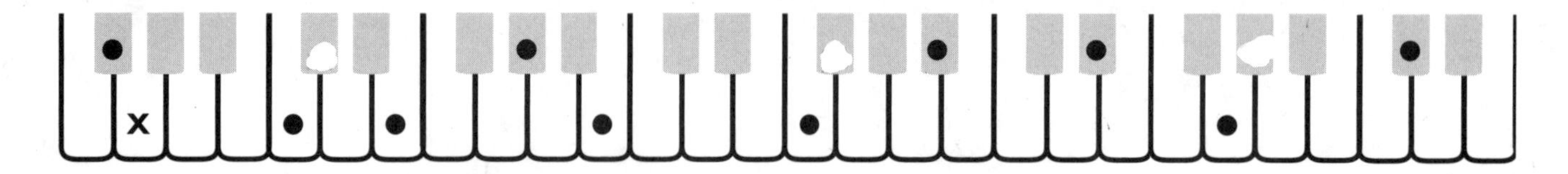

With RH fingers 2-3, play each of the half steps you marked.

For correlated Discoveries, Repertoire and Technic, see MUSIC TREE 2A, pages 10-16.

Whole Steps

A WHOLE STEP is made of two half steps with one key skipped.
Whole steps can look **four** different ways on the keyboard:

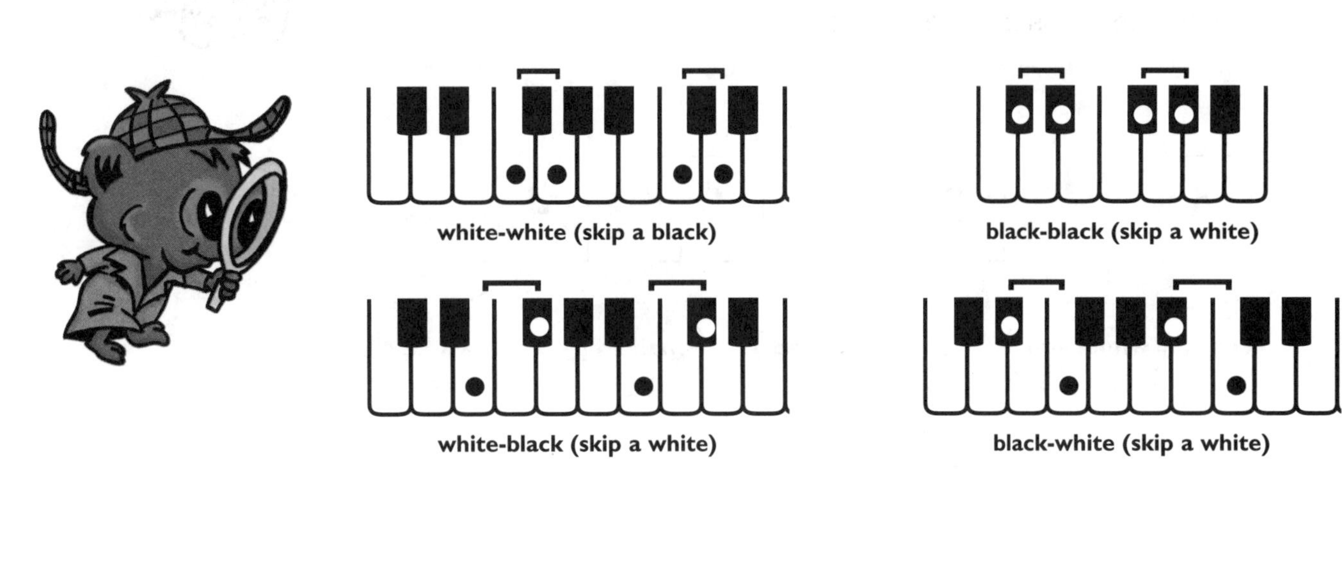

Circle the whole steps in this jumble.

Mark an X on the key a whole step **above** each dotted key.

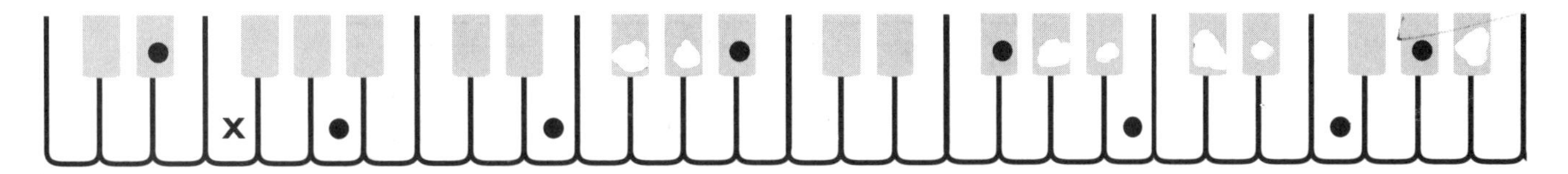

With RH fingers 2-3, play each of the whole steps you marked.

Major 5-Finger Patterns

Major 5-finger patterns are made of 5 tones that use this pattern of whole steps and half steps:

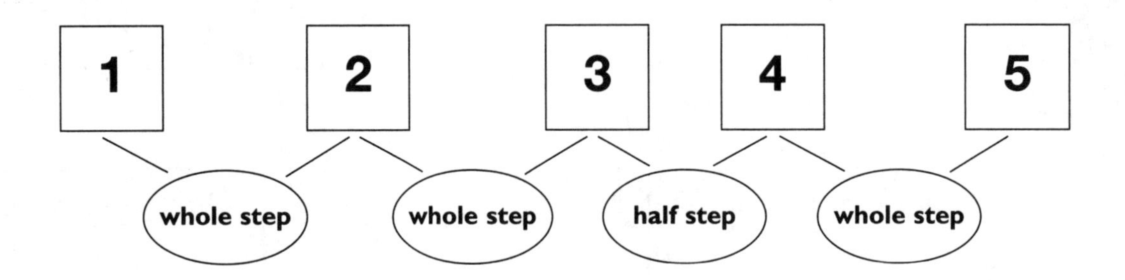

A 5-finger pattern is named by the first tone (degree 1).

For example, the D Major 5-finger pattern is:

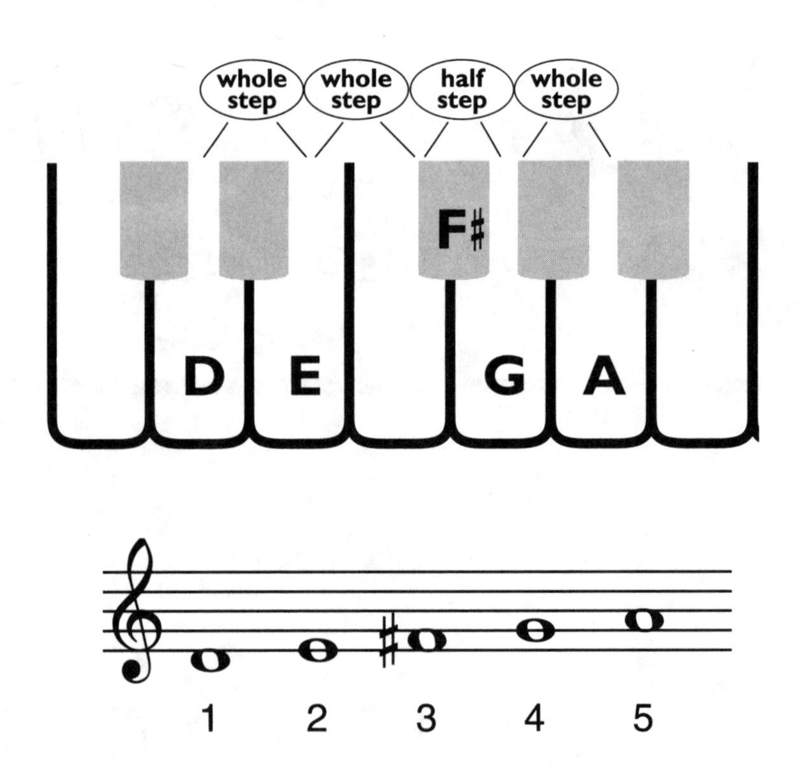

Draw each of these major 5-finger patterns:

On the keyboards, write the letter names.

On the staves, draw whole notes for each of the five tones.

Then, mark the half step with a ‿ .

The first one is done to show you how.

C Major — C D E F G

D Major — D

E Major — E

F Major — F

G Major — G

A Major — A

Rhythm

Walking Eighth Notes

1. Swing and say the rhyme with a strong rhythmic pulse.

Happy Birthday To You

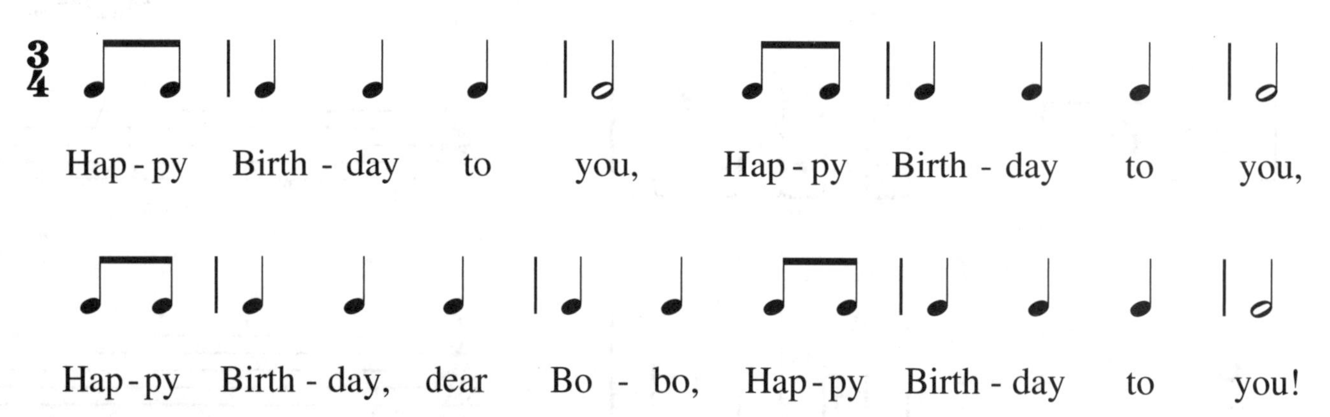

2. Say the rhyme again, making dashes under the words.
3. Walk the rhythm as you say the rhyme, taking one step for each **pulse**.
4. Then walk the rhythm again, taking one step for each **note**.

Counting Eighth Notes

In each of these rhythms, set a strong rhythmic pulse:

1. Point and count.
2. Tap and count (notes **above** the line are for RH, notes **below** the line are for LH).
3. Play and count – RH on G, LH down an octave.

Adventures in Sight-Playing

These pieces are made mainly of 3rds and repeated notes.

By playing the 3rds with fingers 1 and 3 and exchanging fingers on the repeated notes, you can explore higher and lower on the staff than ever before!

Before playing the pieces, practice this exercise until it is smooth and easy.

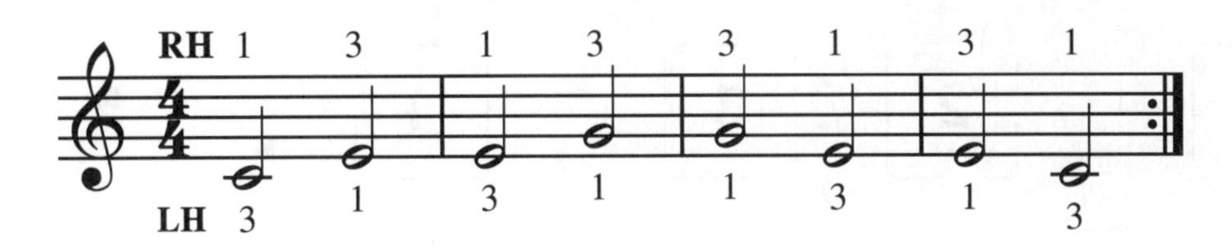

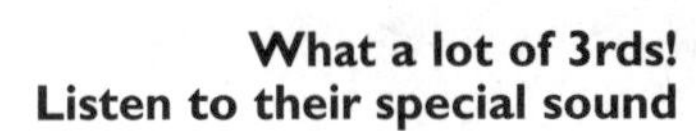

Circle the highest note.

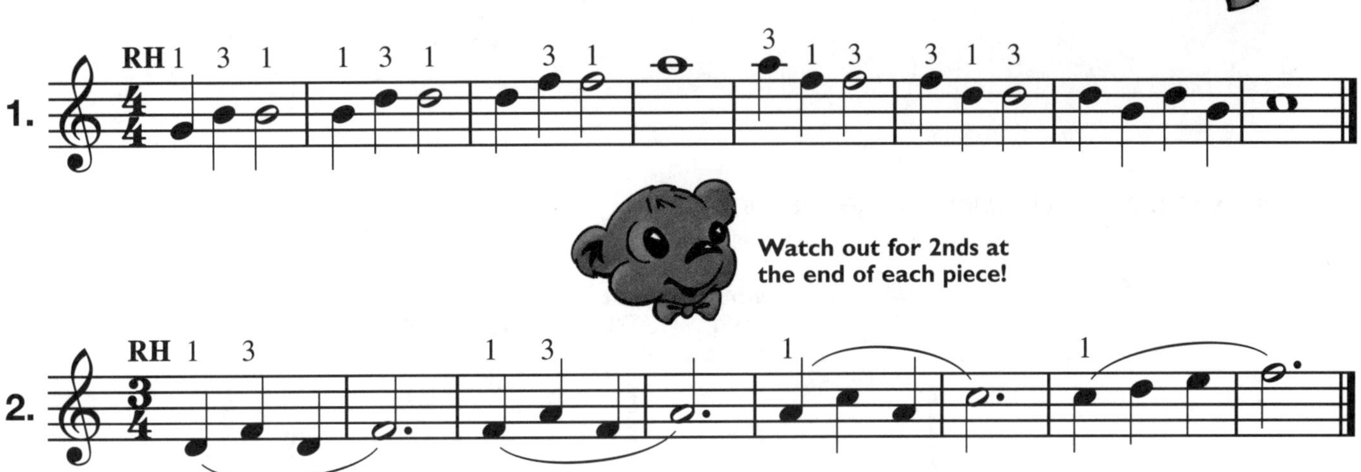

Circle the lowest note.

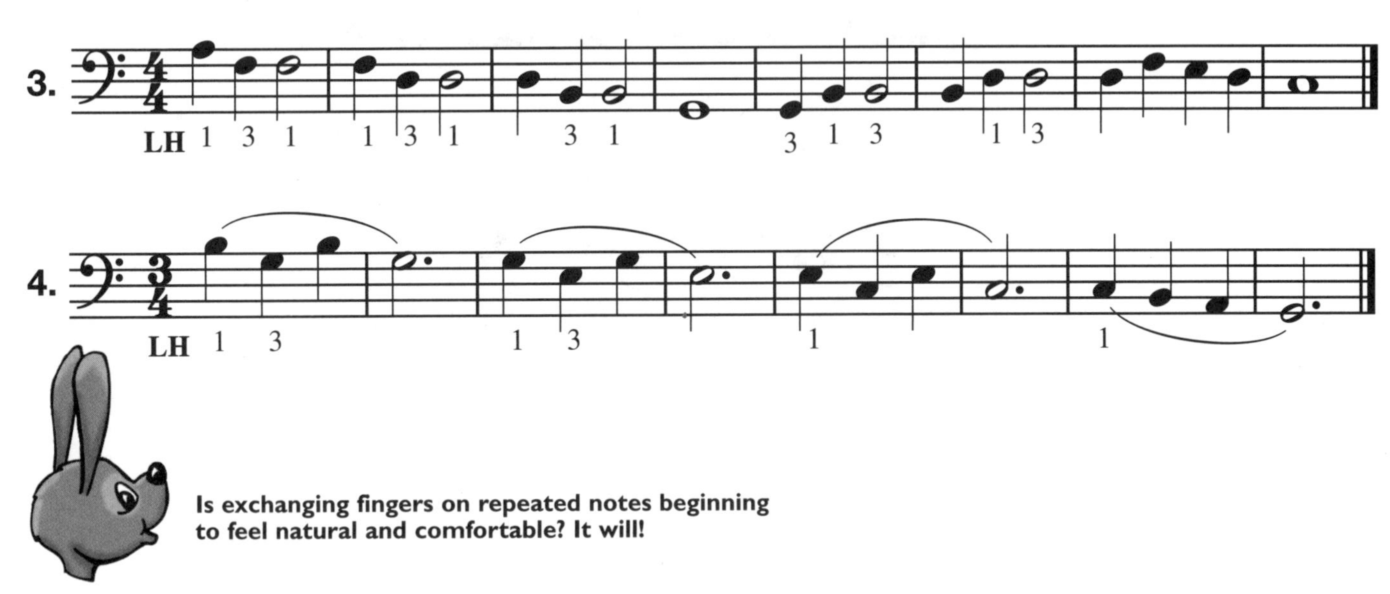

UNIT THREE

Theory

Minor 5-Finger Patterns

In minor 5-finger patterns, a half step occurs between the 2nd and 3rd tones.

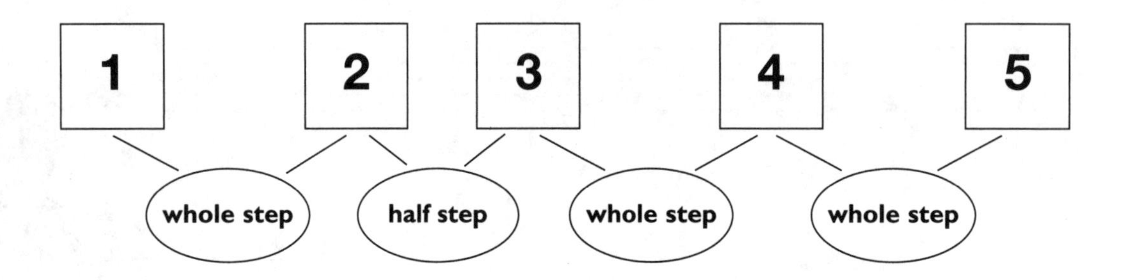

For example, the D Minor 5-finger pattern is:

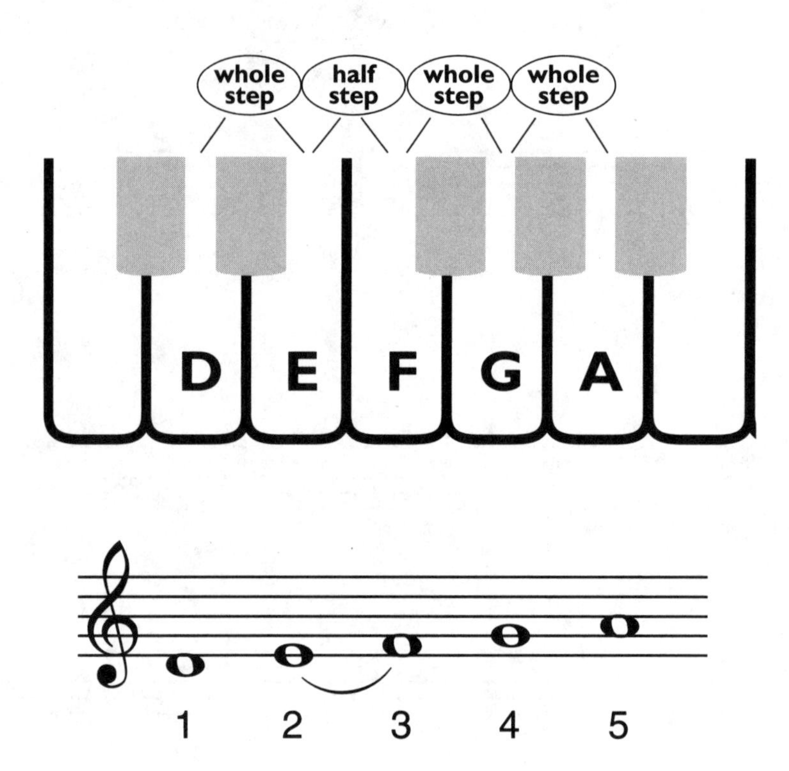

For correlated Discoveries, Repertoire and Technic, see MUSIC TREE 2A, pages 17-23.

Draw each of these minor 5-finger patterns:

On the keyboards, write the letter names.
On the staves, draw whole notes for each of the five tones.

Then, mark the half step with a ‿ .

The first one is done to show you how.

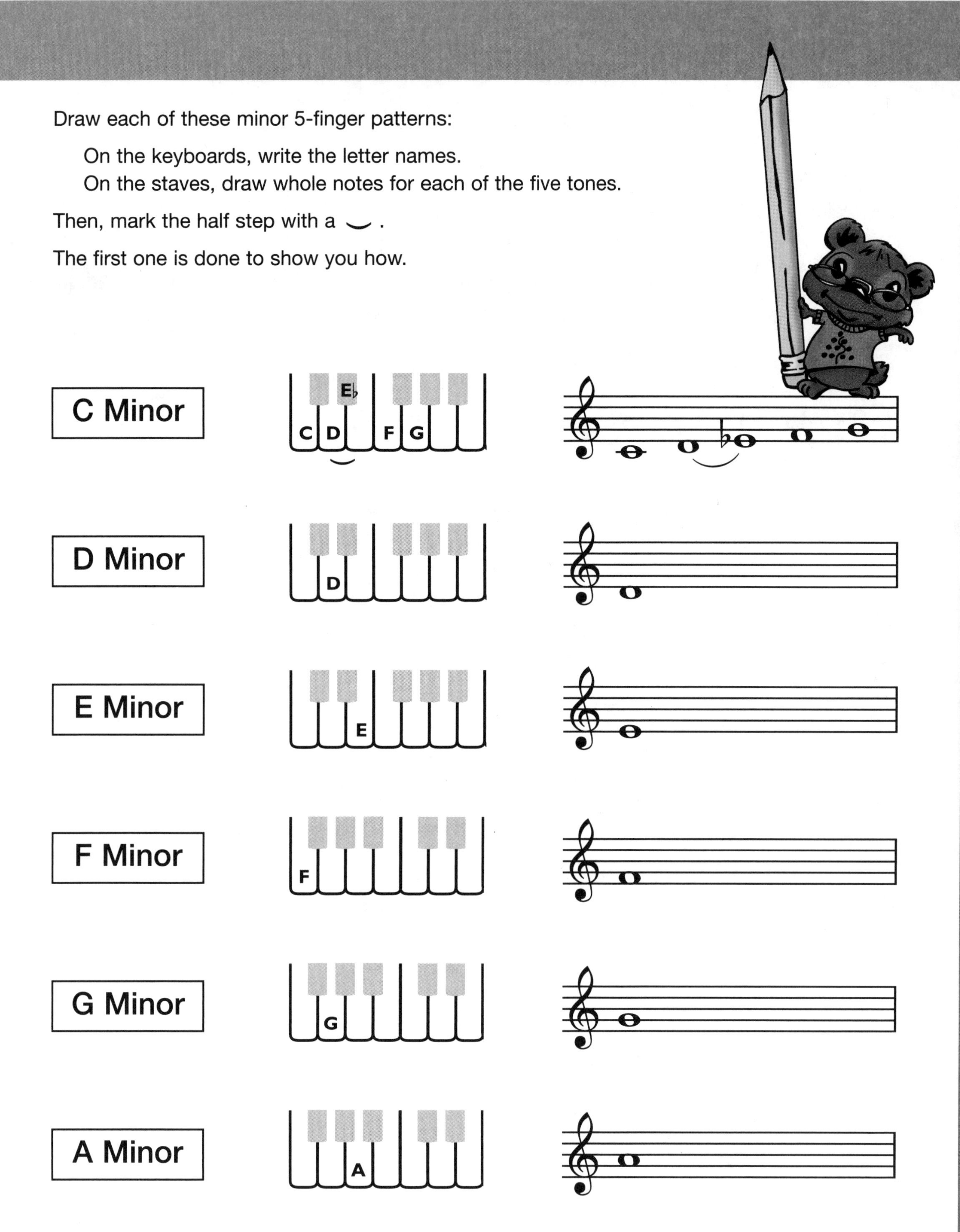

Using Perfect 5ths to Accompany Melodies

You can use the perfect 5th (P5) of any major or minor 5-finger pattern to accompany a melody that uses the notes of that pattern.

When you can play each of these melodies easily:

1. Accompany it with the perfect 5th.
2. Change the melody to minor and play it again with your accompaniment.

Bagpipes uses the notes of the _____ major 5-finger pattern.

Bagpipes

Transpose *Bagpipes* with your accompaniment to G major, then to G minor.

Here is another way to use the P5 as an accompaniment.
Parade uses the notes of the _____ major 5-finger pattern.

Parade

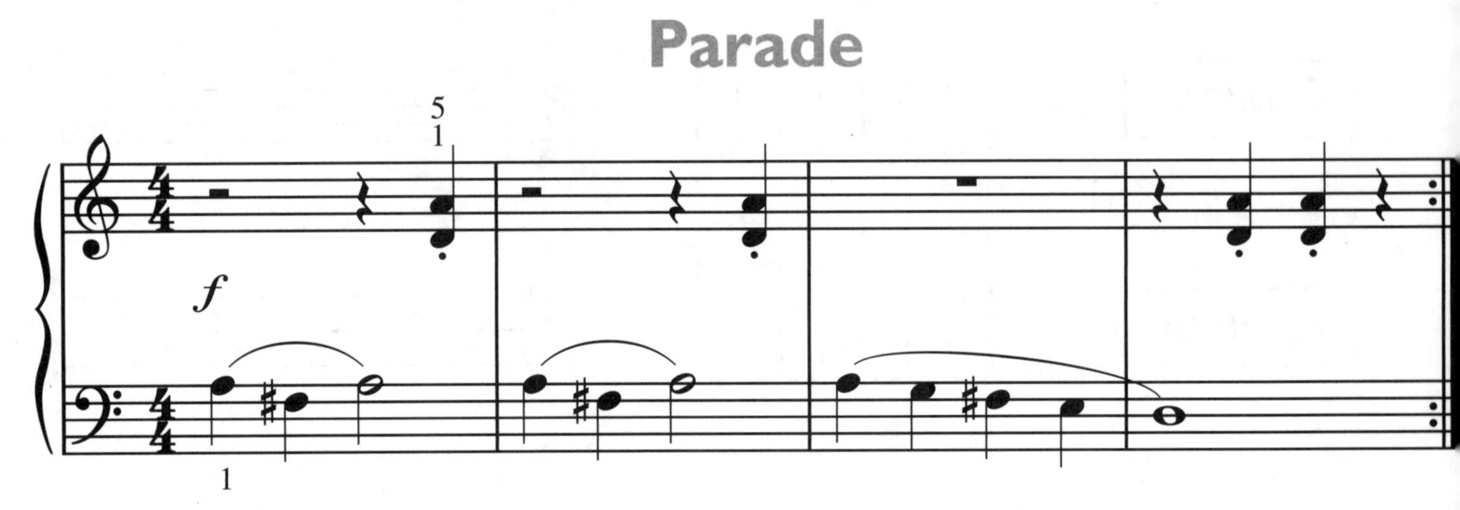

Transpose *Parade* with your accompaniment to F major, then to F minor.

Rhythm

Walking Eighth Notes

1. Swing and say the rhyme with a strong rhythmic pulse.

Sing a Song of Sixpence

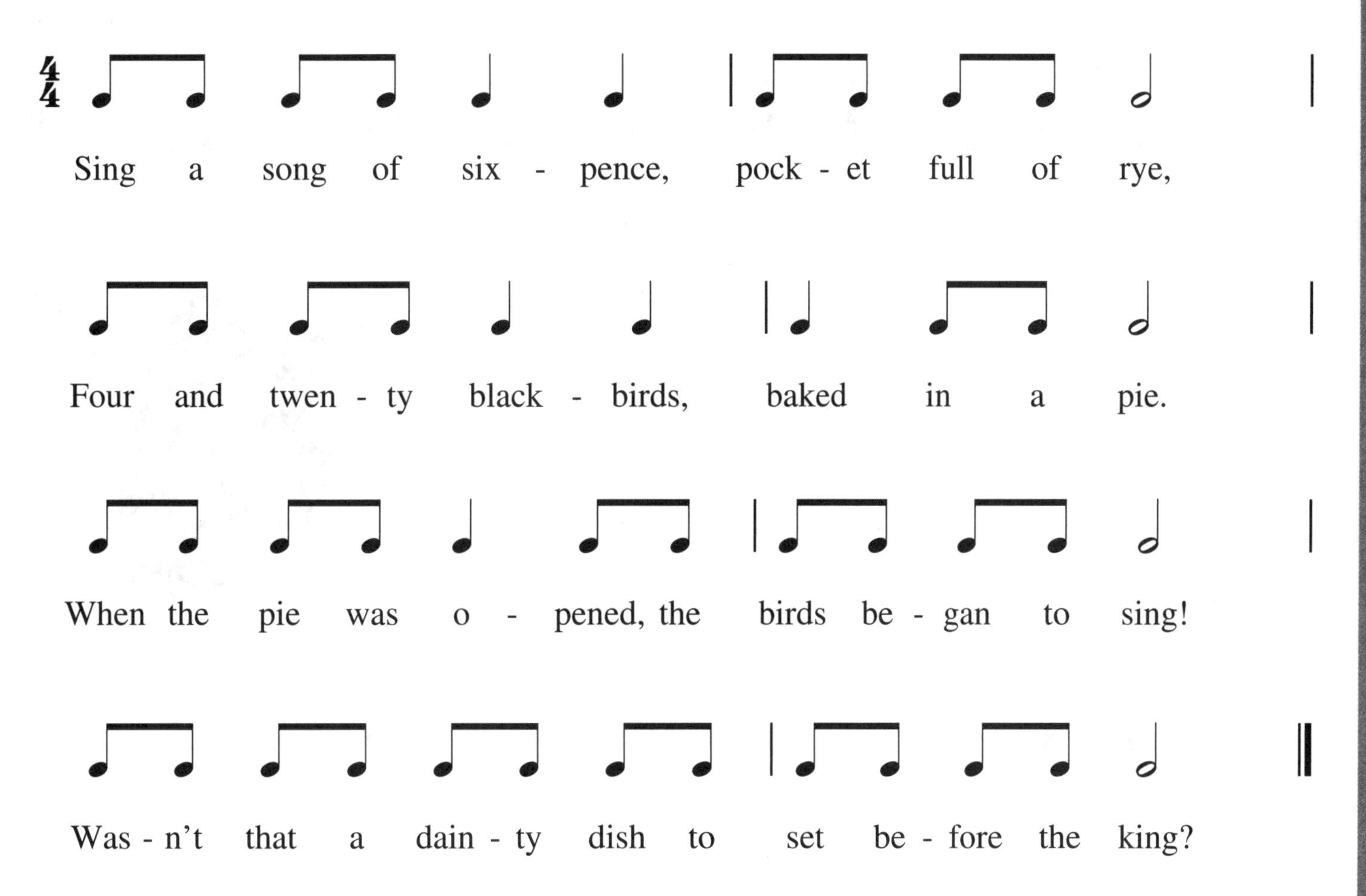

2. Walk the rhythm as you say the rhyme, taking one step for each **pulse**.
3. Walk the rhythm as you say the rhyme again, taking one step for each **note**.

Counting Eighth Notes

In each of these rhythms, set a strong rhythmic pulse:

1. Point and count.
2. Tap and count – one tap for each note.
3. Play and count – RH on B♭, LH on E♭.

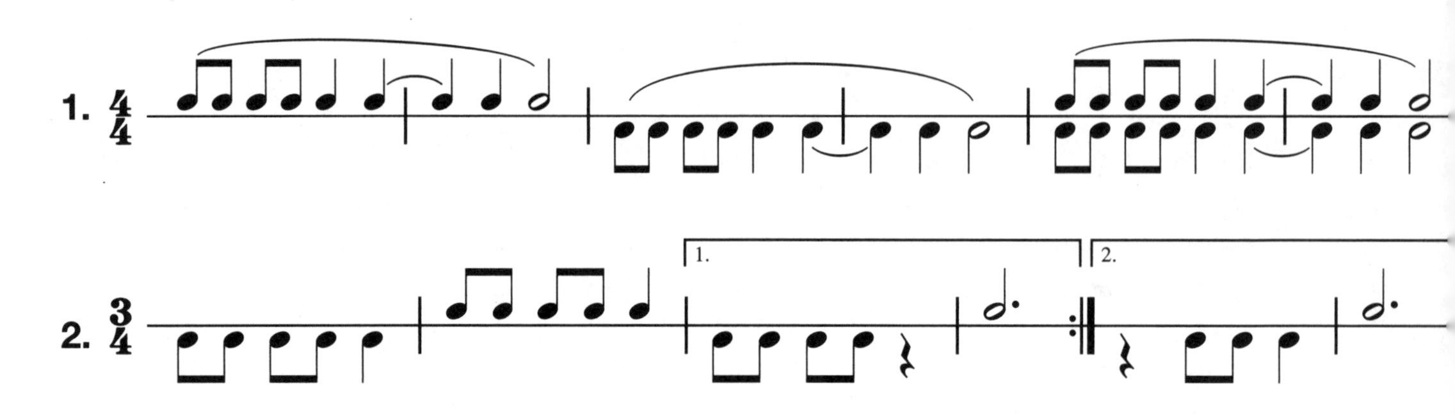

Rhythm Detective

Complete each incomplete measure using one **rest**.

Sight-Playing

1. Circle the clef. Then prepare your hand and fingers on the correct keys.
2. Set a **slow** tempo, counting two measures out loud in a strong rhythmic pulse.
3. Play and count with a full tone, **no stopping** from beginning to end!

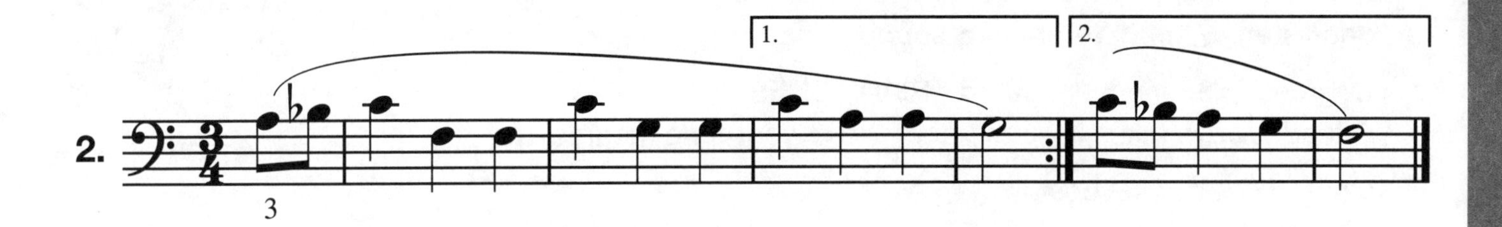

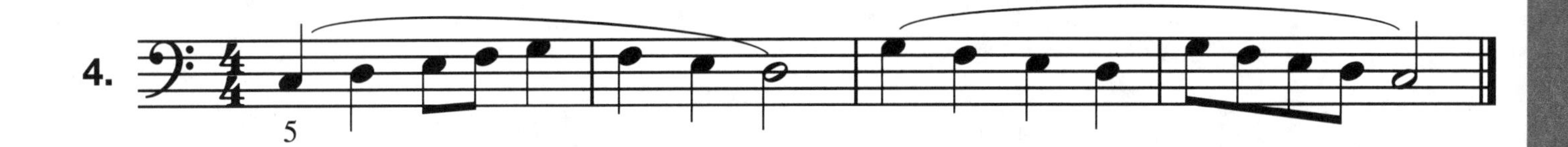

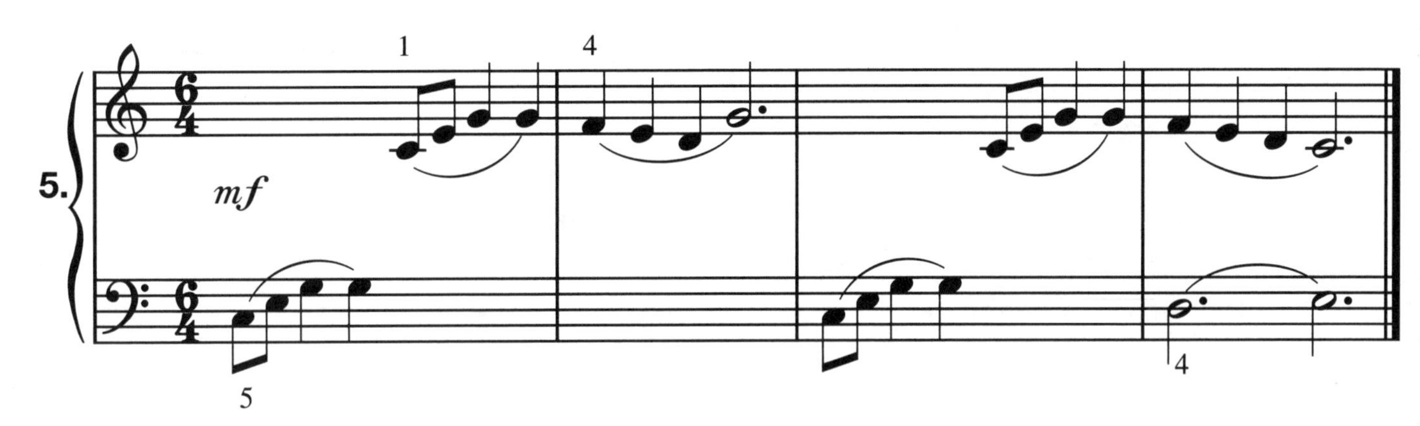

UNIT FOUR

Theory

Major and Minor Triads

Degrees 1, 3, and 5 of any 5-finger pattern form a TRIAD.

In a **major** pattern, they form a MAJOR TRIAD.

In a **minor** pattern, they form a MINOR TRIAD.

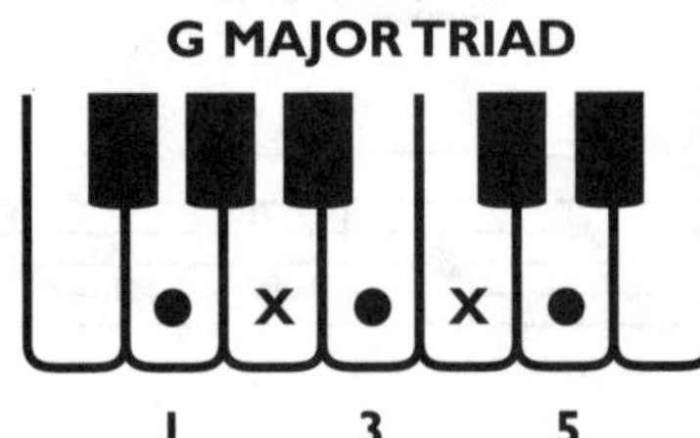

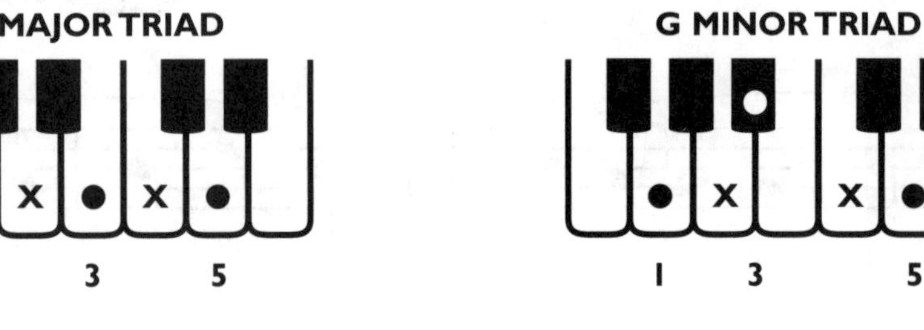

Play the tones of the G major and G minor triads, and listen to the **difference in sound**.

Degrees 1, 3, and 5 are called TRIAD TONES.
A triad always takes its name from the **lowest** tone (degree 1).

On each pair of keyboards:

- Mark the degrees (1, 2, 3, 4, 5) and circle the triad tones.
- Play the triad tones and listen to the sound.
- Mark the triad **M** for major or **m** for minor.

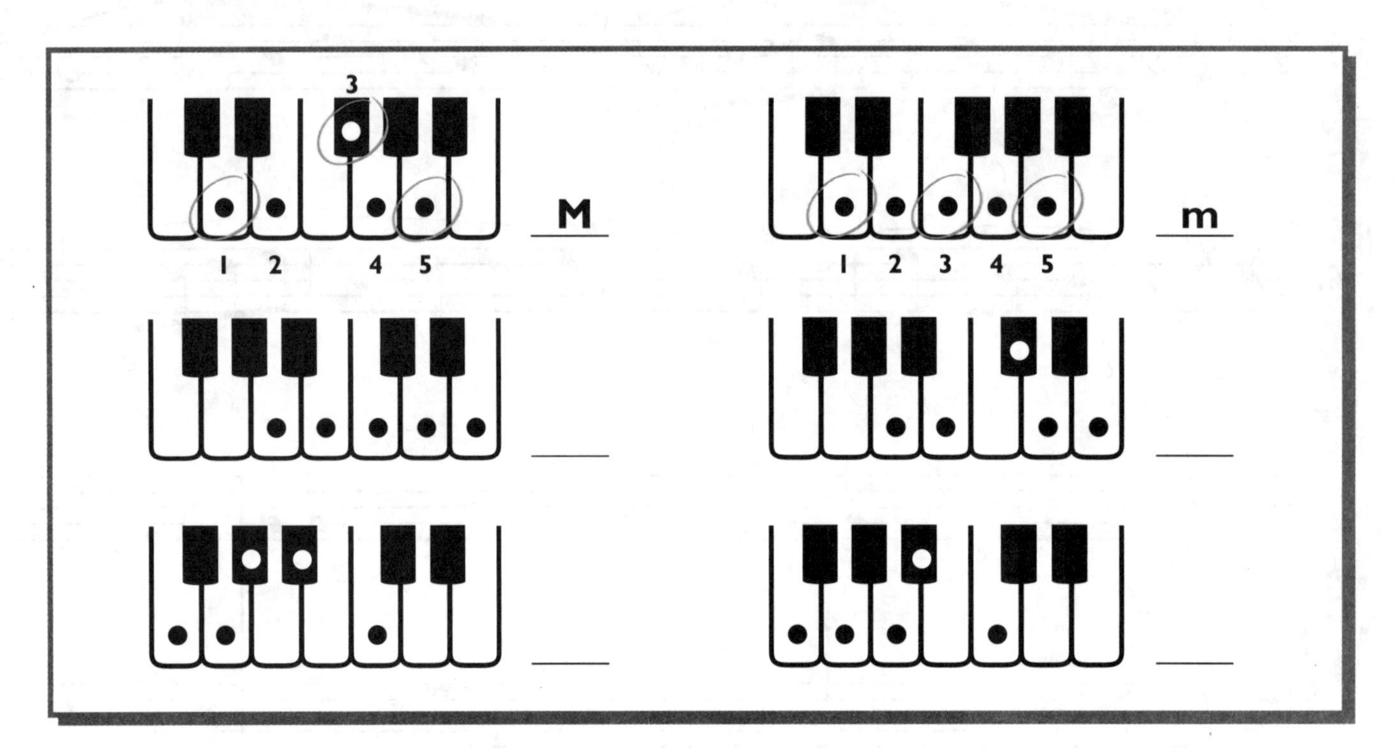

For correlated Discoveries, Repertoire and Technic, see MUSIC TREE 2A, pages 24-29.

Non-Triad Tones

Degrees 2 and 4 are not part of the triad, so they are called NON-TRIAD TONES.

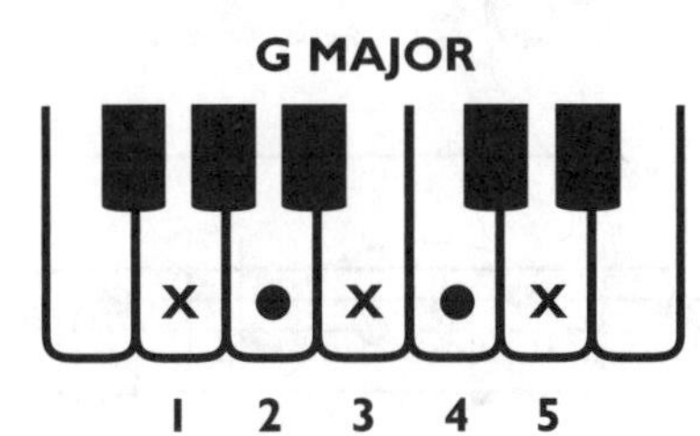

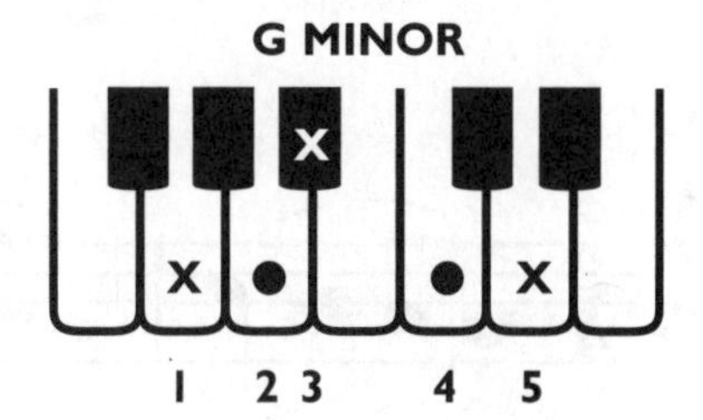

In each example below:

- Circle the **non**-triad tones in each measure.
- Play, and listen to the difference in sound between the triad and non-triad tones.

Accompanying and Transposing

Circle Dance uses the notes of the _____ major five finger pattern.
When you can play the melody easily:
Make an accompaniment for it using the P5.
Then change the melody with its accompaniment to **minor**.

Circle Dance

Transpose *Circle Dance* with your accompaniment to F major, then to F minor.

Rhythm

Walking Eighth Notes

1. Swing and say the rhyme with a strong rhythmic pulse.

At Twilight

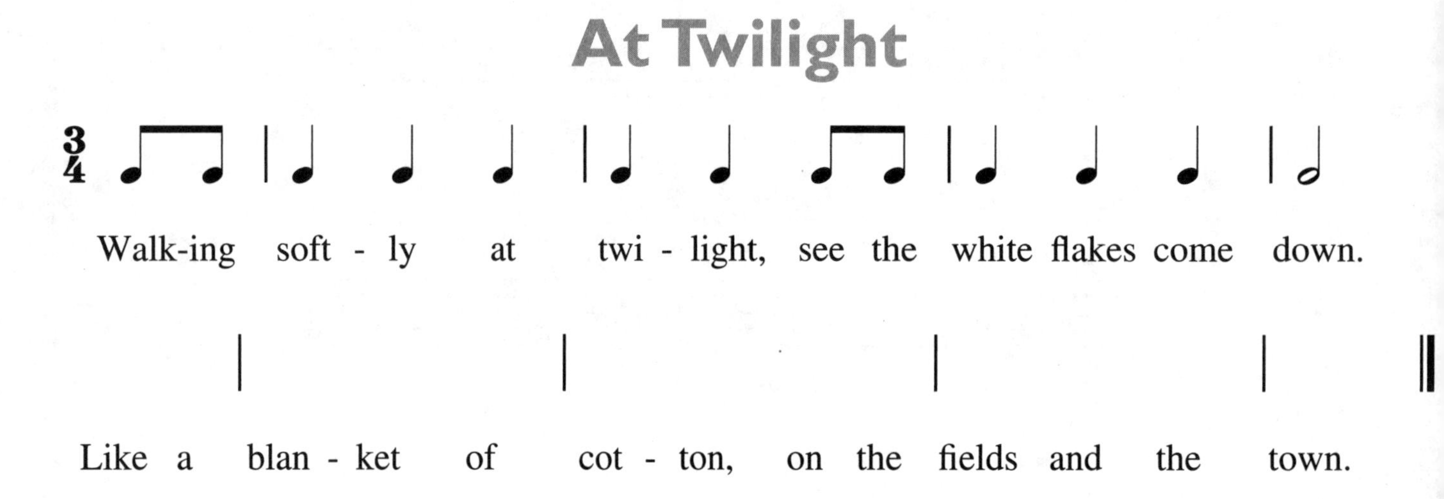

2. Fill in the notes above the last line.
3. Walk the rhythm as you say the rhyme, taking one step for each **pulse**.
4. Walk the rhythm as you say the rhyme again, taking one step for each **note**.

Counting Eighth Notes

In each of these rhythms, set a strong rhythmic pulse:

1. Point and count the RH.
2. Tap and count HT.
3. Play and count — RH on A♯, LH on F♯.

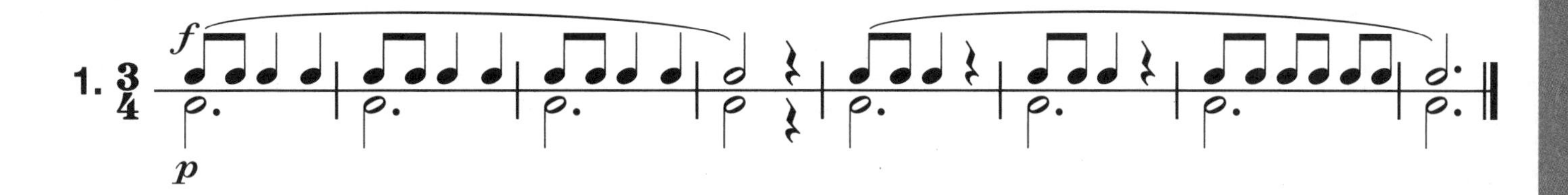

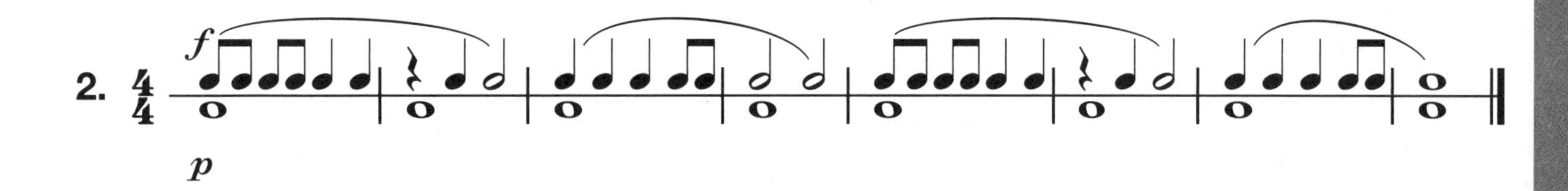

Rhythm Detective

Circle the measures that have too many pulses.

Adventures in Sight-Playing

Still more pieces made mainly of 3rds and repeated notes!

Enjoy reaching all the way to finger 5 before the finger exchange.

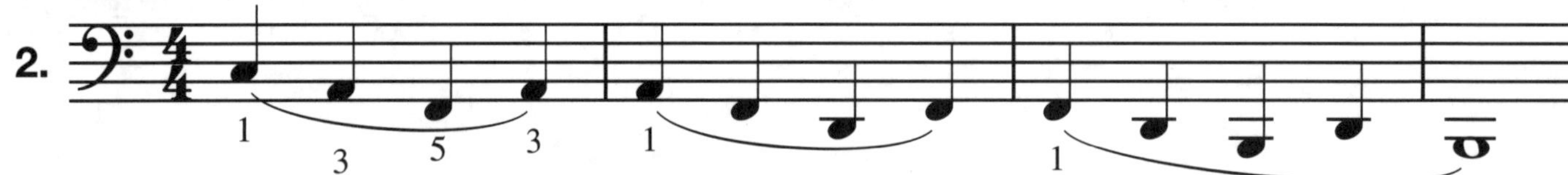

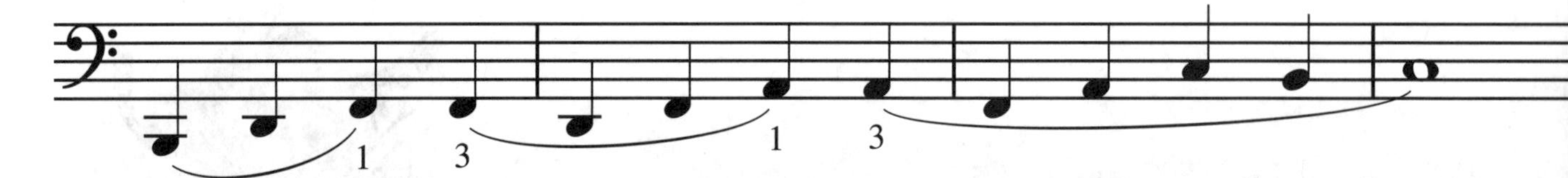

Aren't you surprised you can read notes this low

Aren't you surprised you can read notes this high

Remember — there's no hurry! The important thing is to make a beautiful tone, and to enjoy the loose feeling in your hand and arm.

Follow the Pathway

Begin at the bottom and help Bobo find his way to the top by writing major 5-finger patterns. The last note of the pattern becomes the first note of the next pattern. Remember the sharps and flats!

UNIT FIVE

Theory

Accompanying with Tonic and Dominant

Tonic (**I**) is the name for degree 1 of a 5-finger pattern.

Dominant (**V**) is the name for degree 5 of a 5-finger pattern.

Tonic and Dominant can be used to accompany melodies.

- Tonic accompanies measures where the melody contains triad tones.
- Dominant accompanies measures where the melody contains non-triad tones.

Clog Dance uses the notes of the _____ major 5-finger pattern.

Tonic (**I**) is _____. Dominant (**V**) is _____.

Complete the LH notes for line 2.

- Mark **I** under measures made of triad tones.
- Mark **V** under measures made of non-triad tones.

Then play the melody with your accompaniment.

Clog Dance

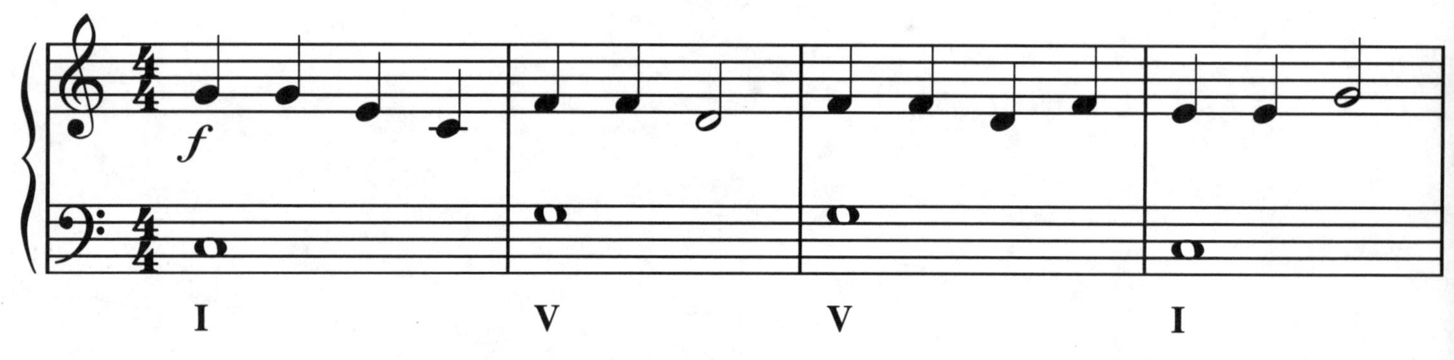

Now transpose *Clog Dance* with your accompaniment to G major.

For correlated Discoveries, Repertoire and Technic, see MUSIC TREE 2A, pages 30-35.

To accompany each of the following melodies:

- Complete the sentence above each melody.
- Mark **I** under measures made of triad tones.
- Mark **V** under measures made of non-triad tones.

Then play the melody with your accompaniment.

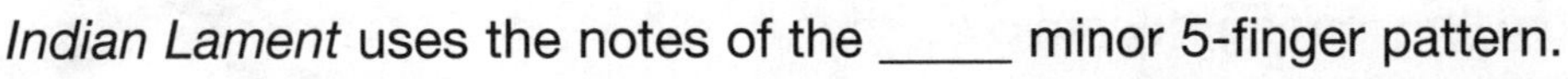

Indian Lament uses the notes of the _____ minor 5-finger pattern.

TONIC (degree **I**) is _____. DOMINANT (degree **V**) is _____.

Indian Lament

Now transpose *Indian Lament* with your accompaniment to C minor.

Folk Dance uses the notes of the _____ major 5-finger pattern.

TONIC (degree **I**) is _____. DOMINANT (degree **V**) is _____.

Folk Dance

Now transpose *Folk Dance* with your accompaniment to A major.

Rhythm

Walking Eighth Notes

1. Swing and say the rhyme with a strong rhythmic pulse.

Peas, Porridge

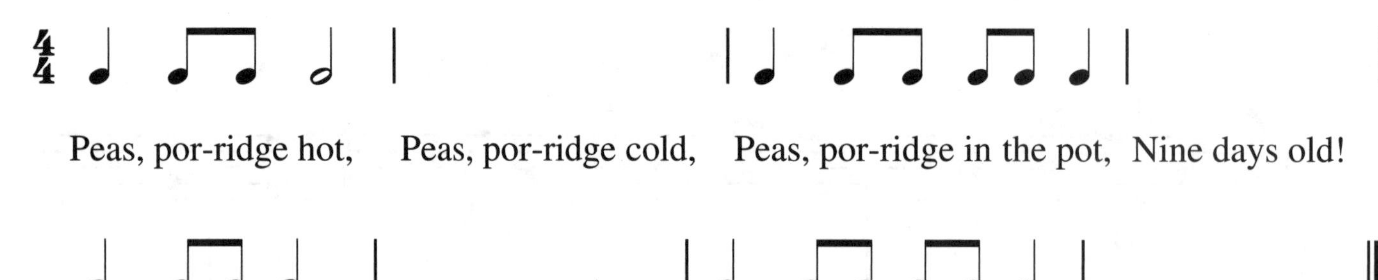

Some like it hot, Some like it cold, Some like it in the pot, Nine days old!

2. Fill in the notes in the empty measures.
3. Walk the rhythm as you say the rhyme, taking one step for each **pulse**.
4. Walk the rhythm as you say the rhyme again, taking one step for each **note**.

Counting Eighth Notes

In each of these rhythms, set a strong rhythmic pulse:
1. Point and count the LH.
2. Tap and count HT.
3. Play and count — LH on C, RH on F.

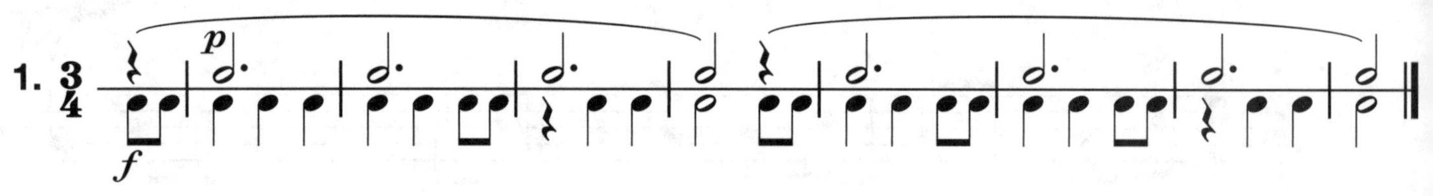

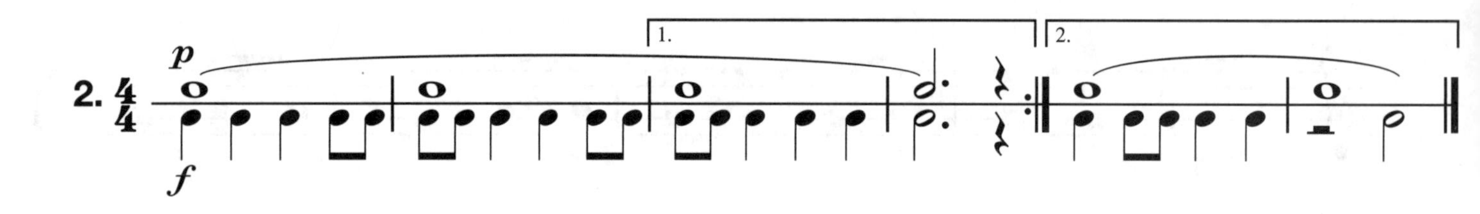

Rhythm Detective

Connect each rhythm pattern to the box with the correct number of pulses.

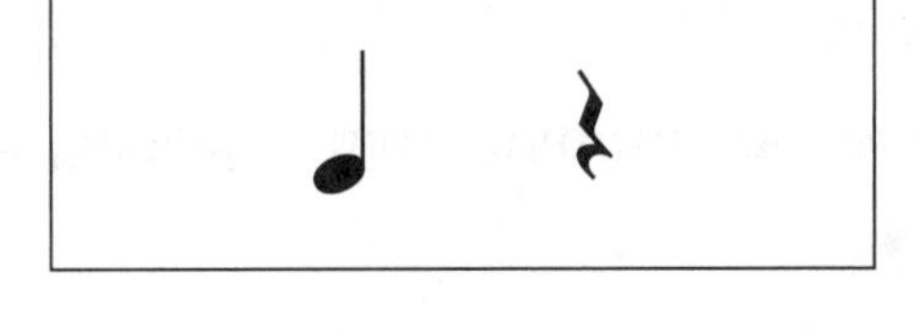

2

3

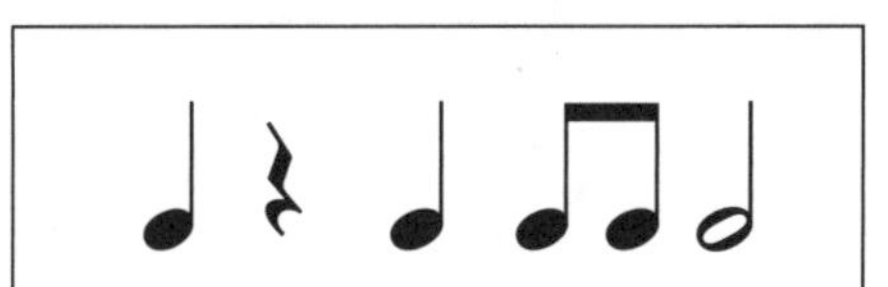

4

6

Sight-Playing

1. Circle the clef. Then prepare your hand and fingers on the correct keys.
2. Set a **slow** tempo, counting two measures out loud in a strong rhythmic pulse.
3. Play and count with a full tone, **no stopping** from beginning to end!

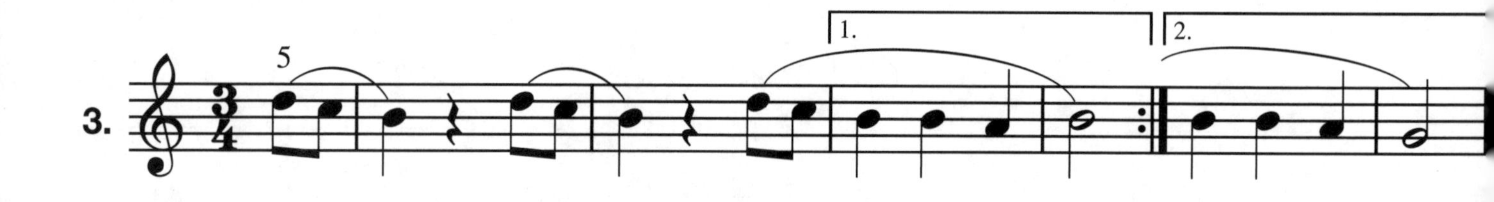

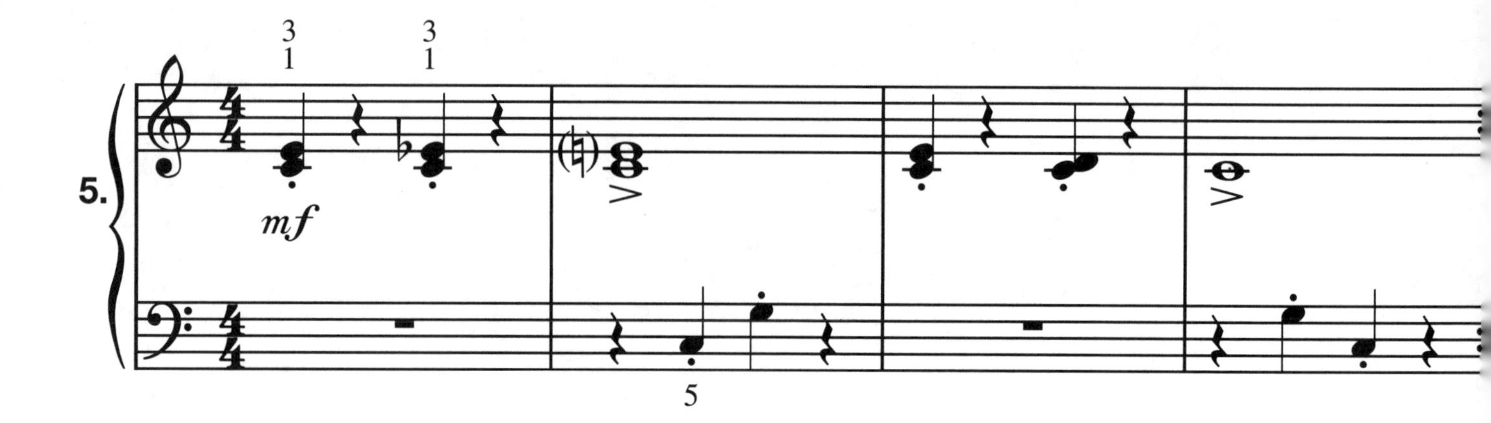

Matching

Draw a line to connect each sign with its name.

major triad
whole step
major five-finger pattern
1st and 2nd ending
tonic
perfect 5th
pedal
minor five-finger pattern
accent
dominant
eighth notes
half step
minor triad

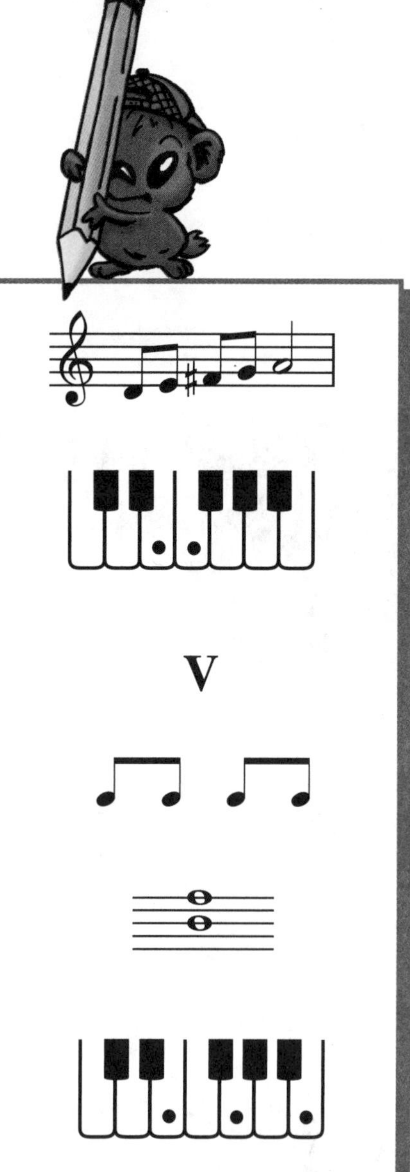

Decoding

Here's a sentence written in code.
To decode the secret message, go back one letter in the alphabet.
For example, every B in the code becomes A and every C becomes B.
Can you solve the message?

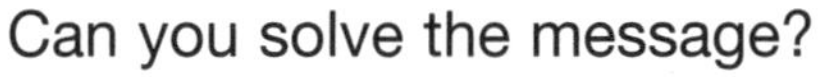

U I

T U

Z P V

O

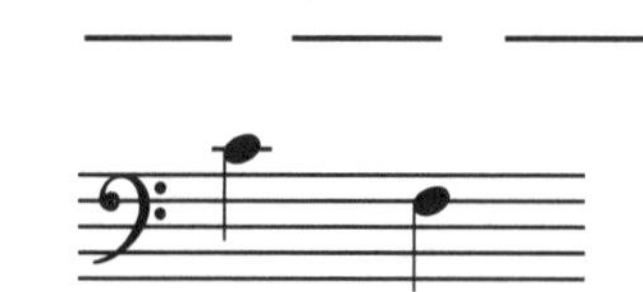

!

Reading

Two New Landmarks: Low F and High G

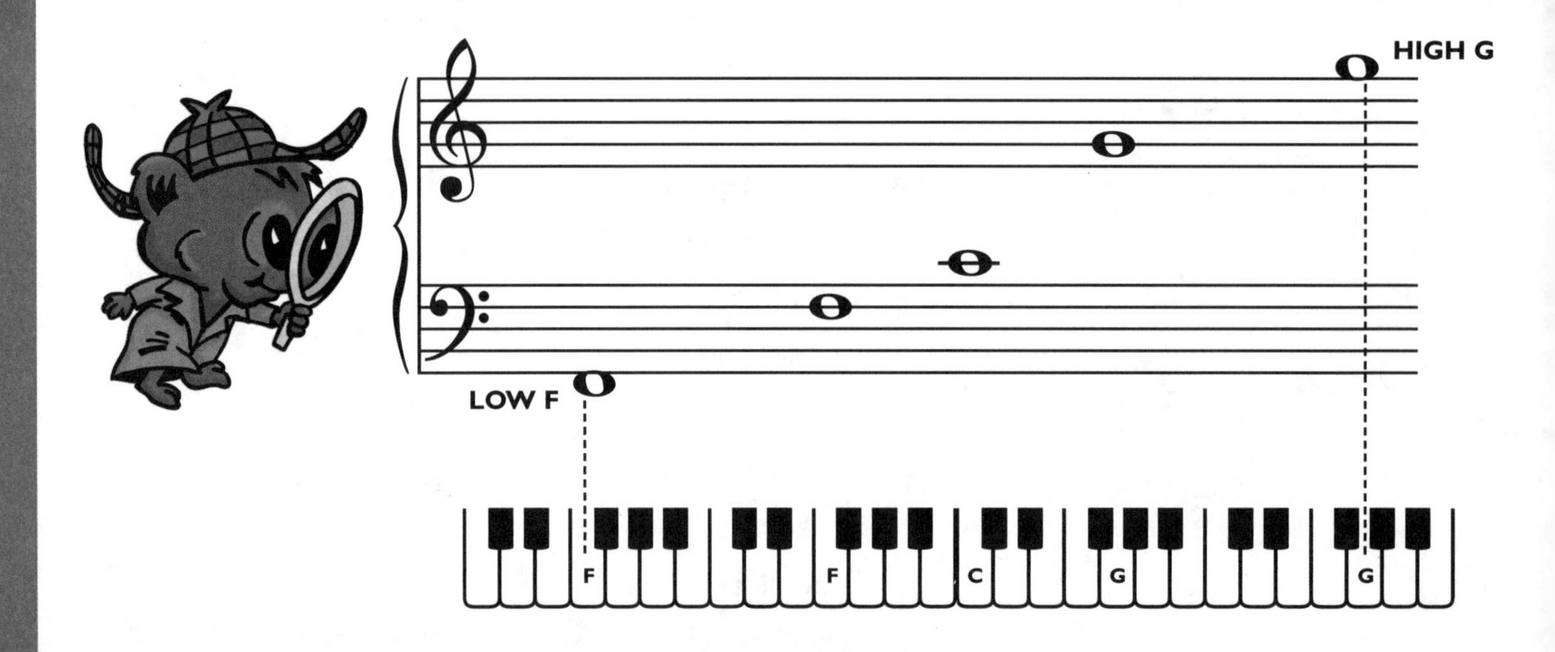

Fill in all the G's. Then circle the **High G's**.

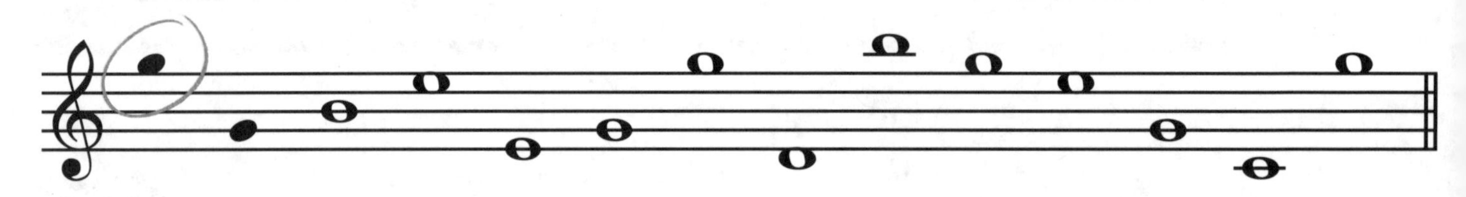

Fill in all the F's. Then circle the **Low F's**.

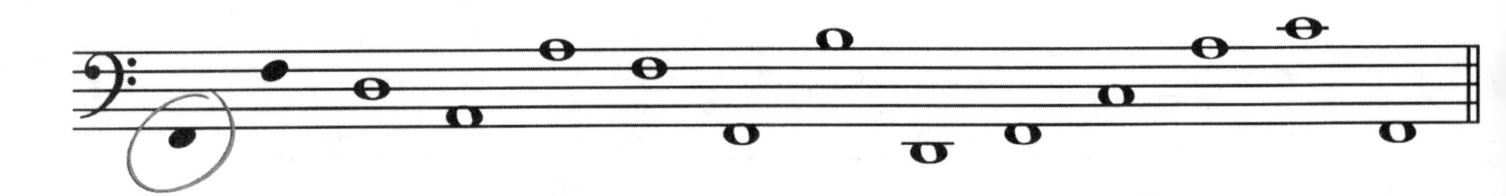

For correlated Discoveries, Repertoire and Technic, see MUSIC TREE 2A, pages 36-41.

Play and name these notes **down** from High G.

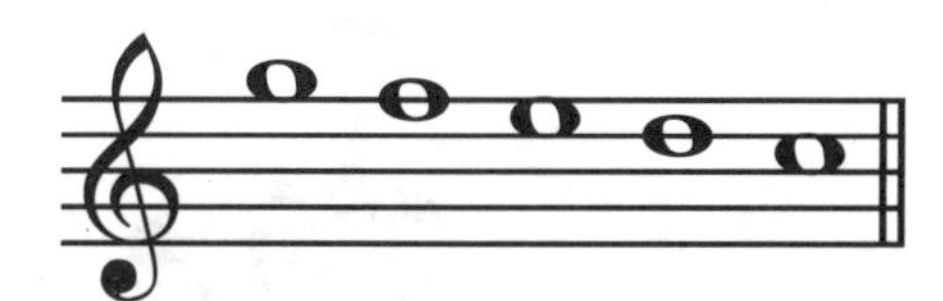

Play and name these notes **up** from High G.

Mark the intervals (3, 4, 5).
Then point and say the direction and interval ("G, down a 3rd, etc.").

Play and name these notes **up** from Low F.

Play and name these notes **down** from Low F.

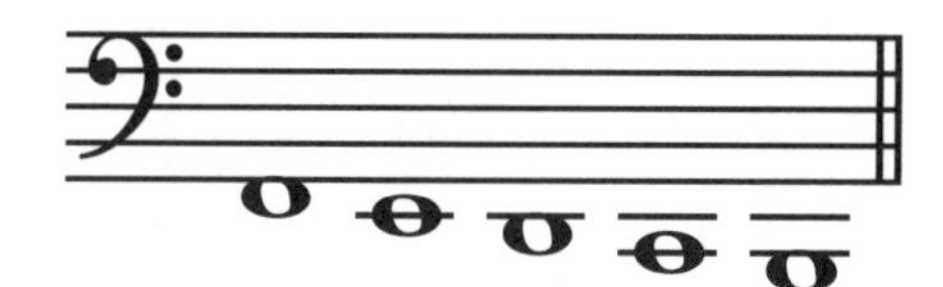

Mark the intervals (3, 4, 5).
Then point and say the direction and interval ("F, up a 3rd," etc.).

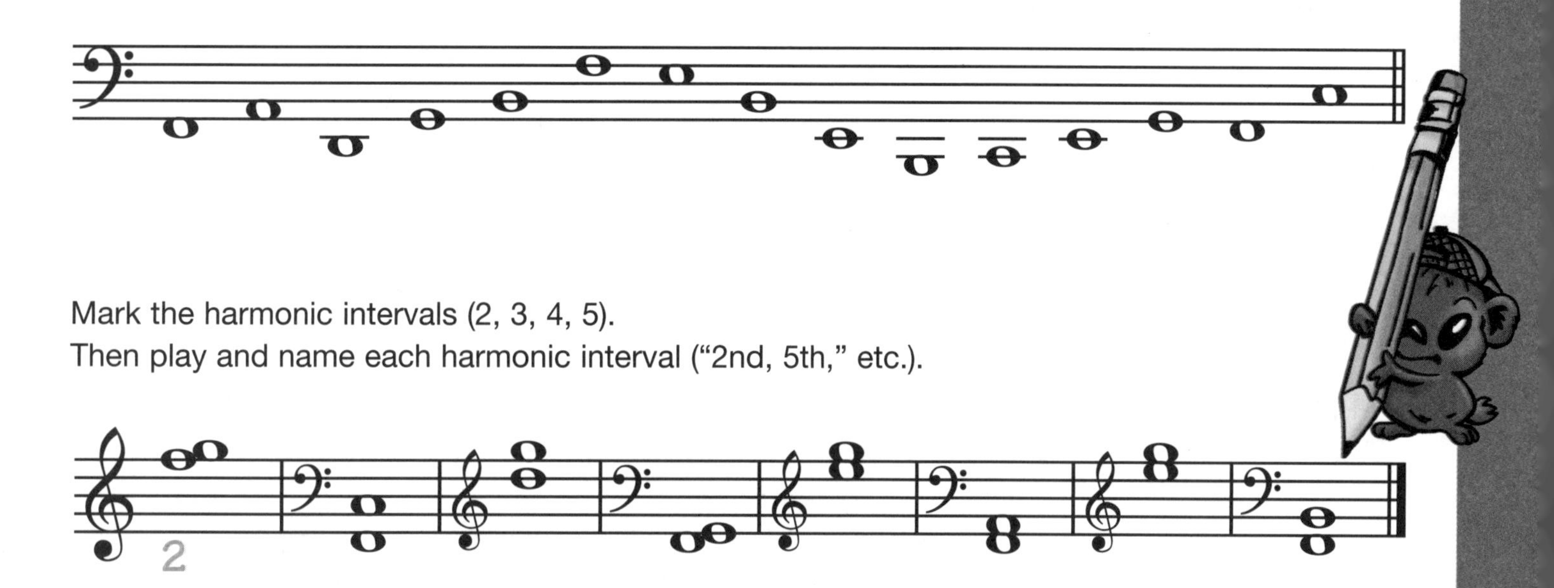

Mark the harmonic intervals (2, 3, 4, 5).
Then play and name each harmonic interval ("2nd, 5th," etc.).

Theory

Accompanying and Transposing

When you can play each melody easily:

- Complete the sentences above each melody.
- Mark **I** under measures made mainly of triad tones.
- Mark **V** under measures made mainly of non-triad tones.

Then play the melody with your accompaniment.

Go Tell Aunt Rhody uses the notes of the _____ major 5-finger pattern.
TONIC (degree **I**) is _____. DOMINANT (degree **V**) is _____.

Go Tell Aunt Rhody

American

Now transpose *Go Tell Aunt Rhody* with your accompaniment to D major.

Slightly Sad uses the notes of the _____ minor 5-finger pattern.
TONIC (degree **I**) is _____. DOMINANT (degree **V**) is _____.

Slightly Sad

Bohemian

Now transpose *Slightly Sad* with your accompaniment to C minor.

Rhythm

Walking Eighth Notes

1. Swing and say the rhyme with a strong rhythmic pulse.

Springtime

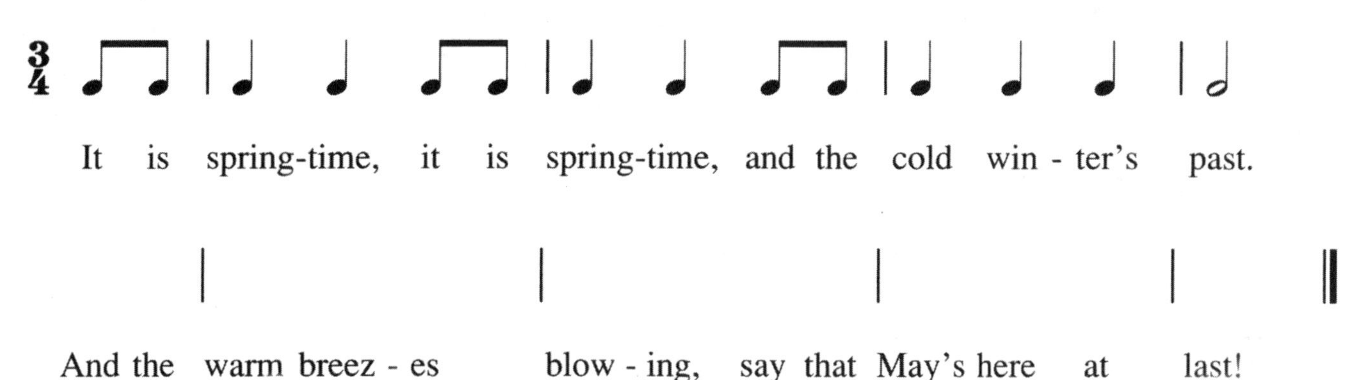

2. Fill in the notes above the second line.
3. Walk the rhythm as you say the rhyme, taking one step for each **pulse**.
4. Walk the rhythm as you say the rhyme again, taking one step for each **note**.

Counting Eighth Notes

In each of these rhythms, set a strong rhythmic pulse:

1. Point and count the melody hand.
2. Tap and count HT.
3. Play and count — RH on C♯, LH on G♯.

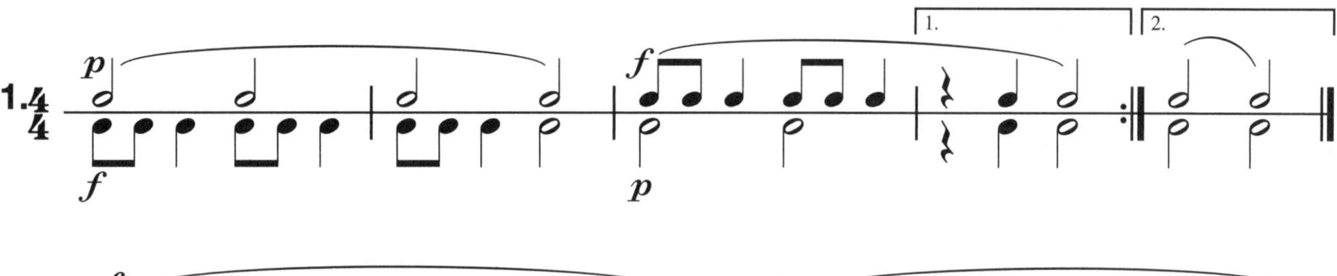

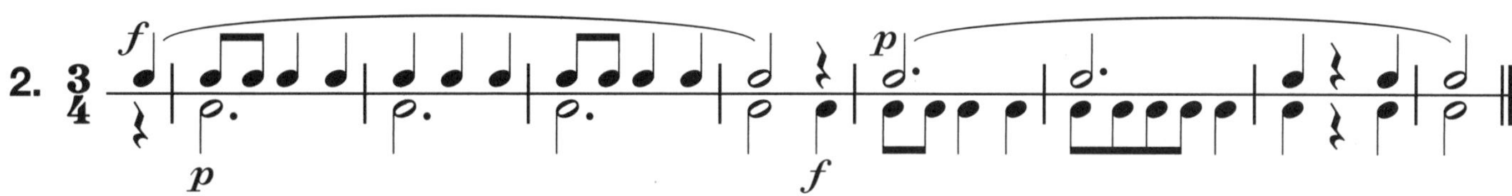

Adventures in Sight-Playing

These *Adventures* begin to use 4ths.
Before playing the pieces, practice this exercise until it is smooth and easy.

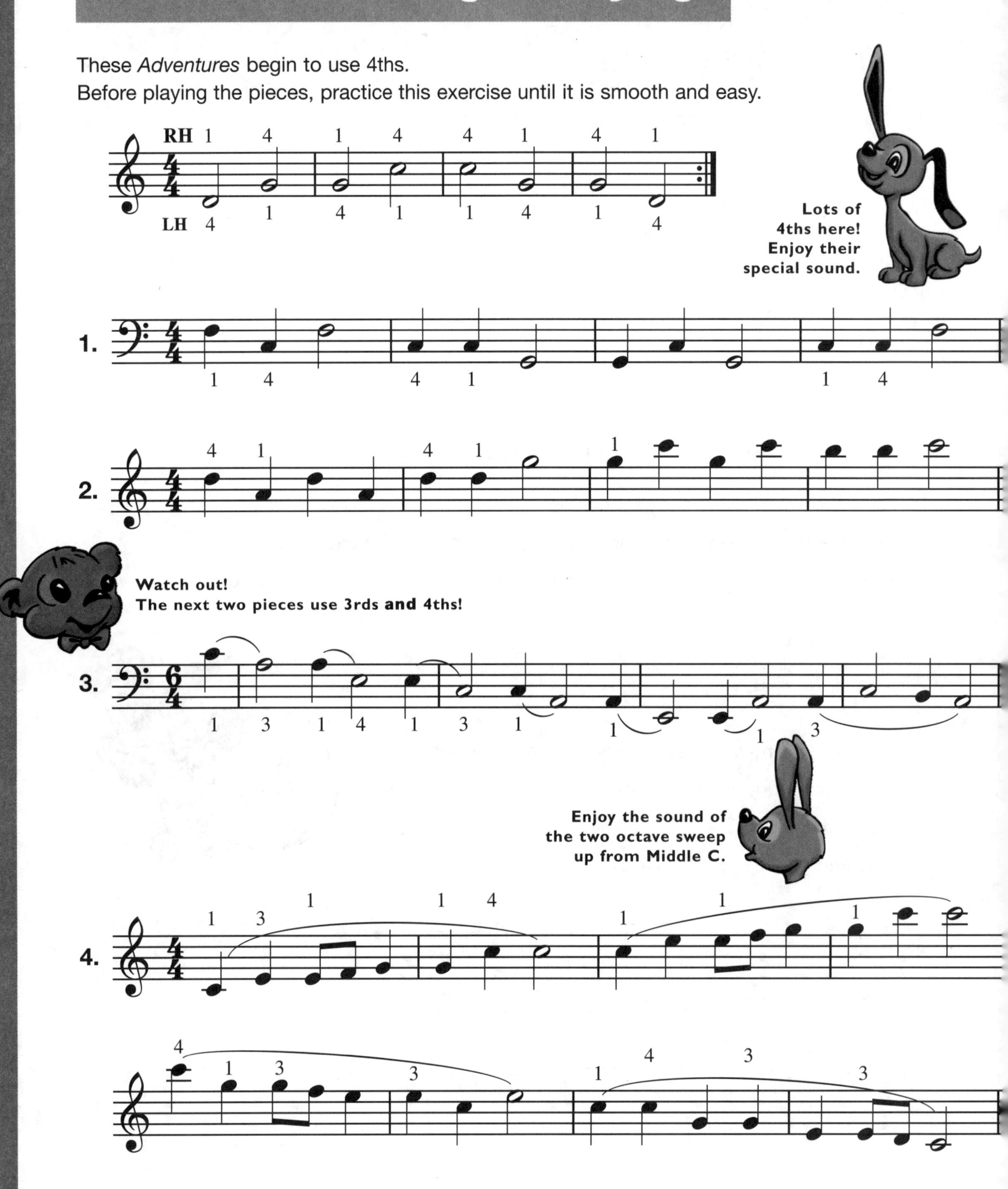

Word Chain

Identify each example, using one letter in each circle.
The last letter of one answer becomes the first letter of the next.

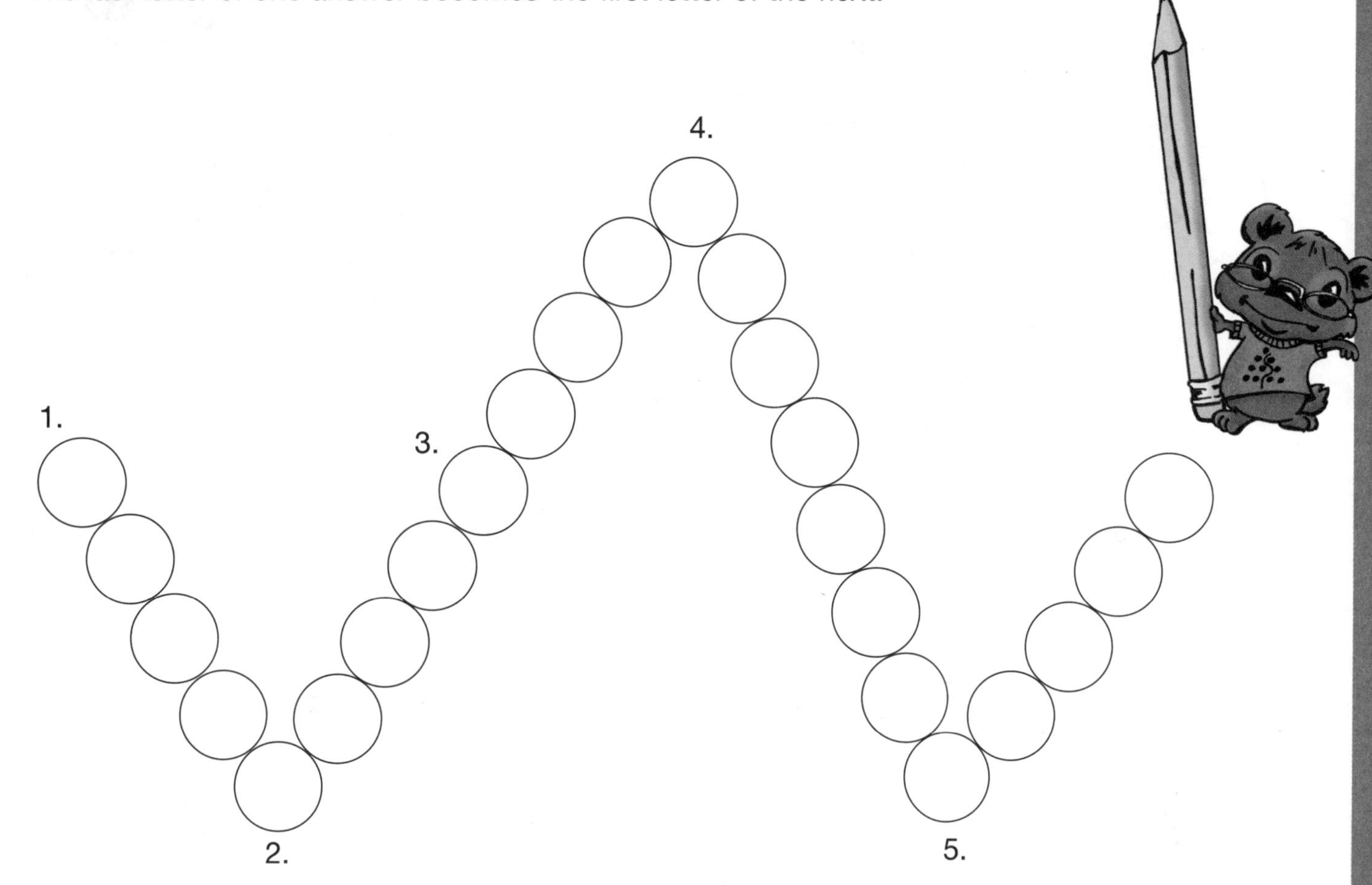

1. **I**

2. C Major 5-finger pattern

3. G Minor 5-finger pattern

4. **V**

5. 

Reading

Naming Notes

Circle the correct music for each group of letter names.

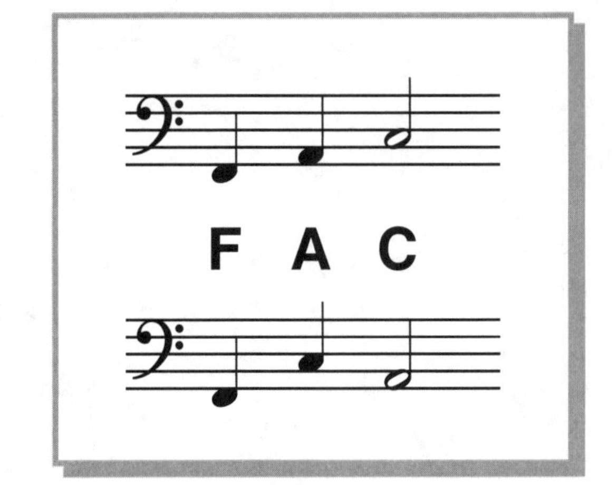

For correlated Discoveries, Repertoire and Technic, see MUSIC TREE 2A, pages 42-47.

Spot-Placing around High G and Low F

Spot-placing is finding a note from the nearest Landmark.

For example, to find this note:

Put an X on the nearest Landmark and name the note, “high G, up a 4th, C.”

(High G space)

Notes around High G

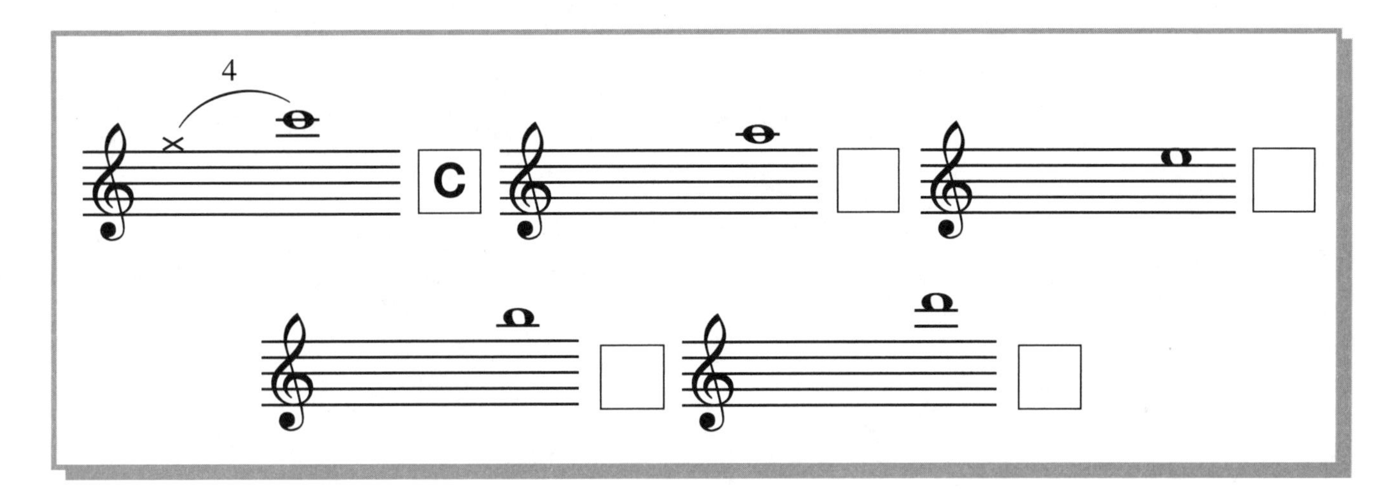

Notes around Low F

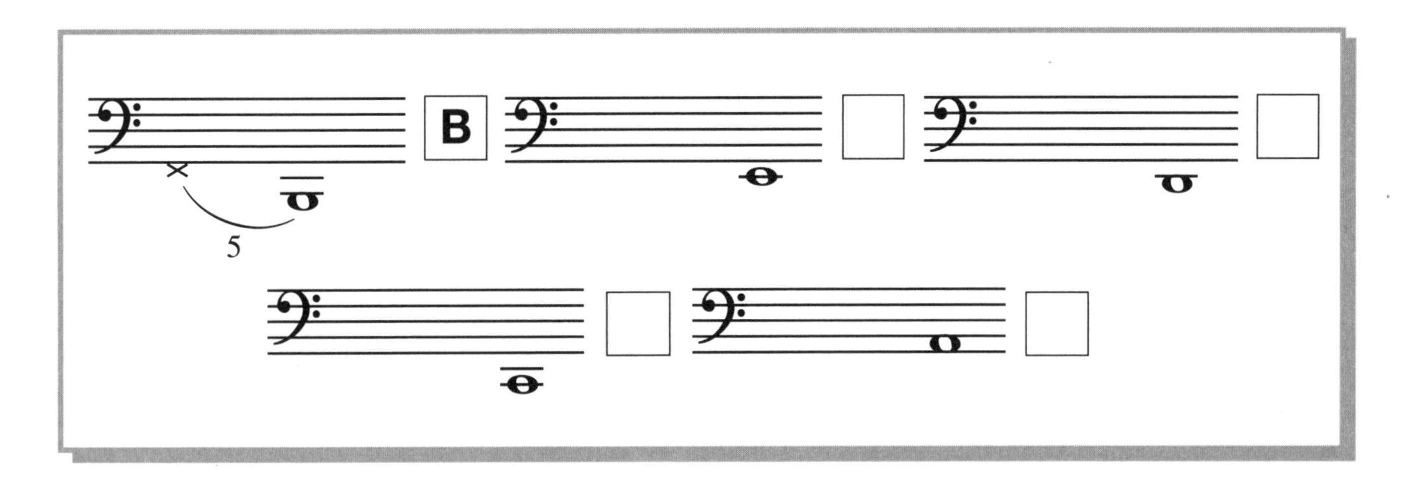

Theory

Accompanying and Transposing

When you can play each melody easily:

- Complete the sentences above the melody.
- Mark **I** under measures made mainly of triad tones.
- Mark **V** under measures made mainly of non-triad tones.

Then play the melody with your accompaniment.

Stamp Dance uses the notes of the _____ major 5-finger pattern.

TONIC (degree **I**) is _____. DOMINANT (degree **V**) is _____.

Stamp Dance

Now transpose *Stamp Dance* with your accompaniment to F major.

Swirling Fog uses the notes of the _____ minor 5-finger pattern.

TONIC (degree **I**) is _____. DOMINANT (degree **V**) is _____.

Swirling Fog

Now transpose *Swirling Fog* with your accompaniment to C minor.

Rhythm

In each of these rhythms, set a strong rhythmic pulse:

1. Point and count hands separately.
2. Tap and count hands together.
3. Play and count — LH on B♭, RH an octave higher.

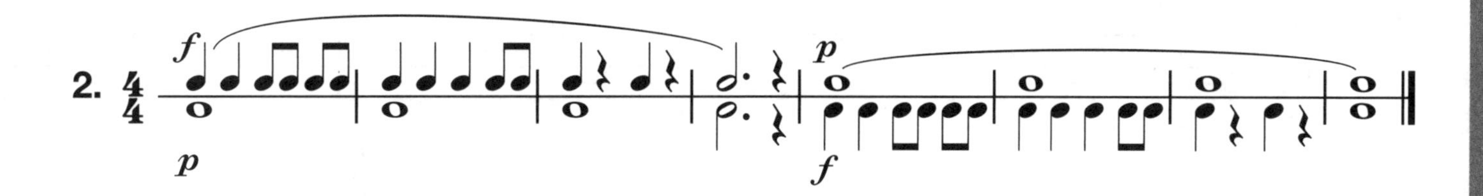

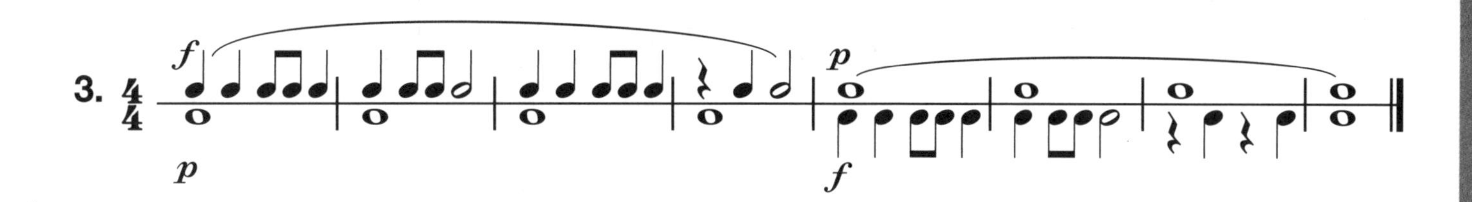

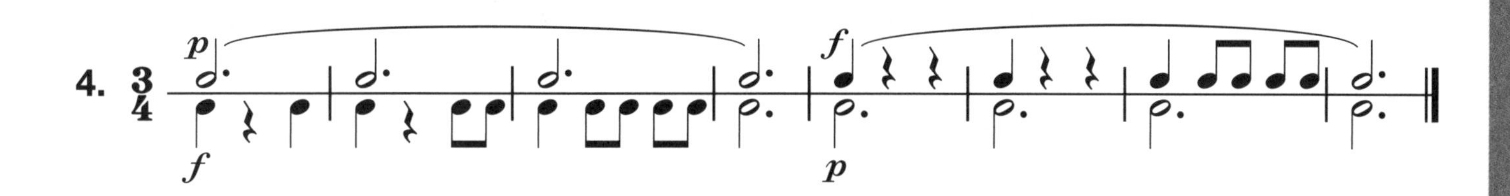

Sight-Playing

Word Search

Circle the words that name each symbol in this puzzle.
The words may go forward, backward, up, down, or diagonally.

1. ♫
2. ♮
3. ♯
4. ♭
5. 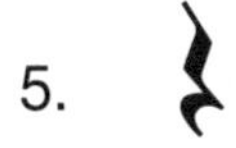
6.
7.
8. I
9. V
10. 

I	I	T	S	E	R	E	L	O	H	W
E	I	G	H	T	H	N	O	T	E	S
F	Q	U	H	I	A	N	N	T	L	H
I	U	A	R	G	L	O	W	F	A	A
R	A	T	E	R	F	T	I	E	D	R
S	R	T	E	R	R	E	S	S	E	P
T	T	E	W	I	E	E	T	O	P	D
E	E	G	A	R	S	T	E	A	P	P
N	R	D	N	A	T	U	R	A	L	L
D	R	D	O	M	I	N	A	N	T	F
I	E	P	E	T	S	E	L	O	H	W
N	S	O	L	W	H	O	T	E	E	N
G	T	O	N	I	C	H	Q	U	A	R

UNIT EIGHT

Reading

Spot-Placing around High G and Low F

To find each of these notes:

- Put an X on the Landmark line.
- Spot-place the note.
- Write its name in the box — then play and name the note.

Notes around High G

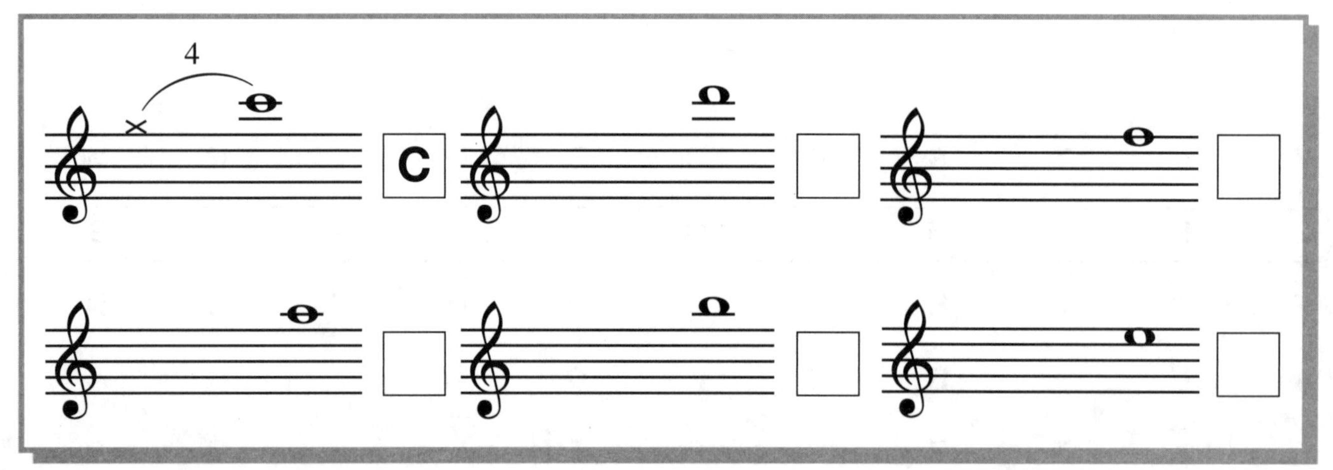

Notes around Low F

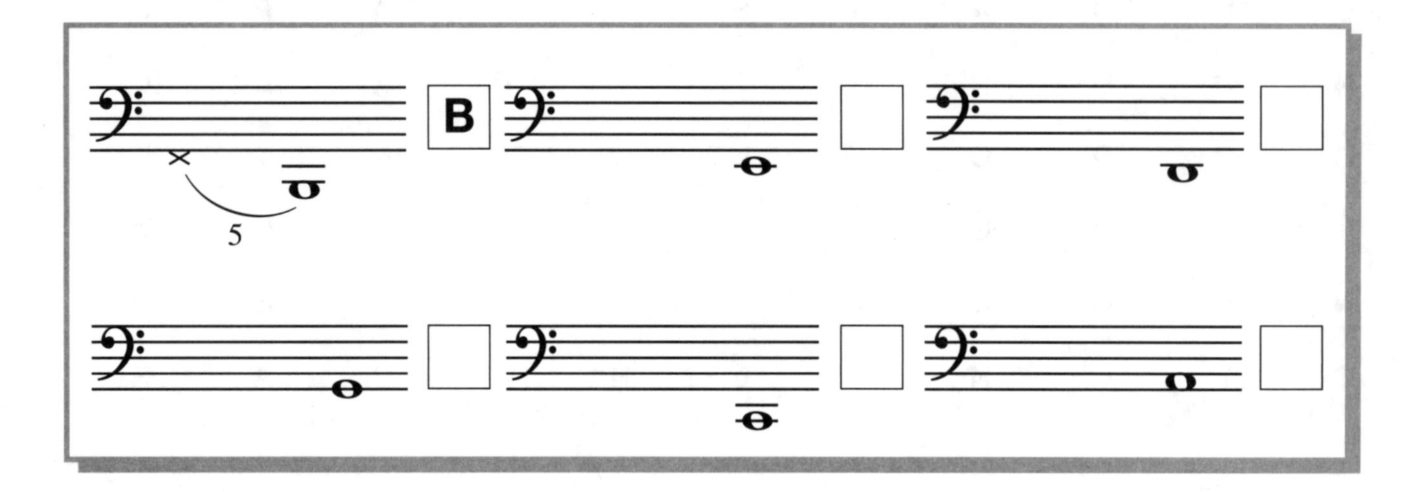

For correlated Discoveries, Repertoire and Technic, see MUSIC TREE 2A, pages 48-53.

Playing Intervals around High G and Low F

Mark the intervals.
Spot-place the first note.
Then play and say the direction, intervals, and note names.

Each hand begins on thumb or 5th finger.

1.

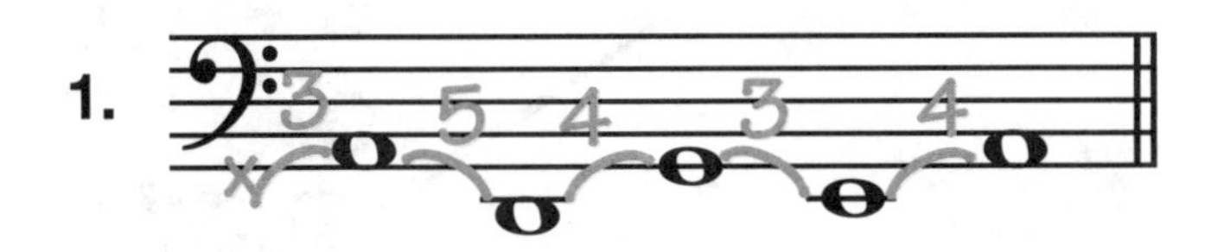

2.

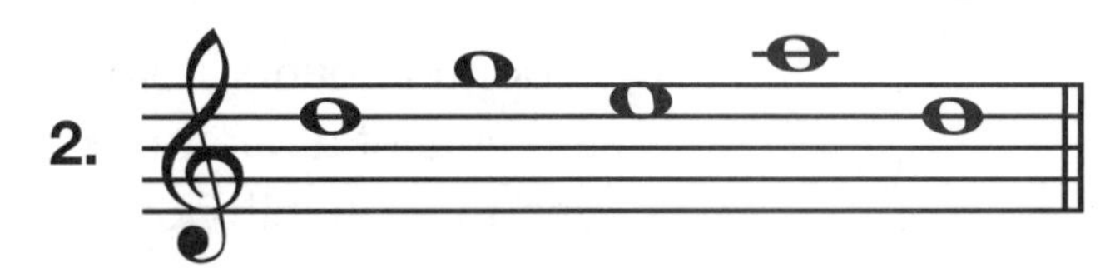

3.

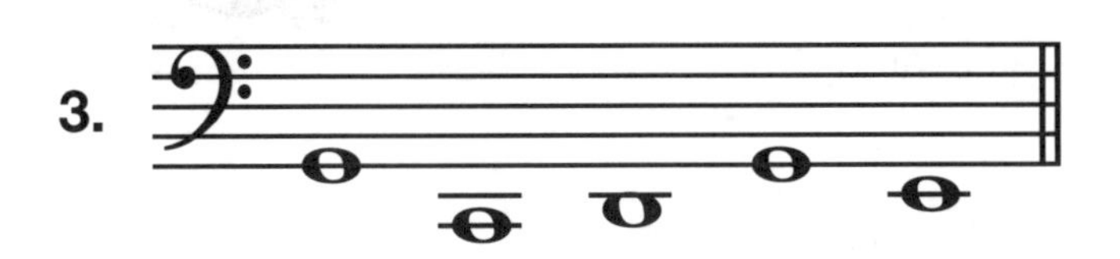

4.

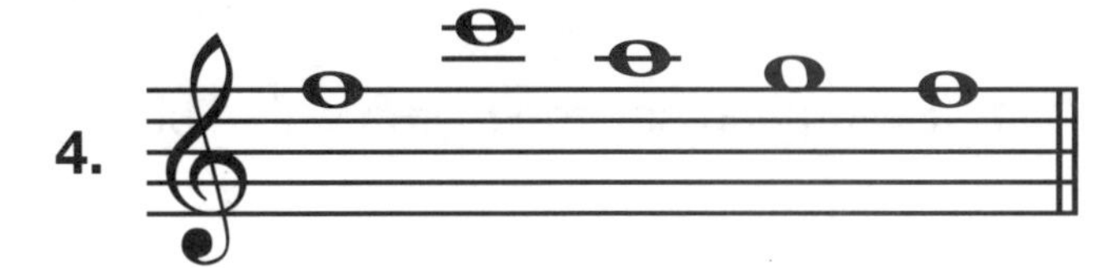

5.

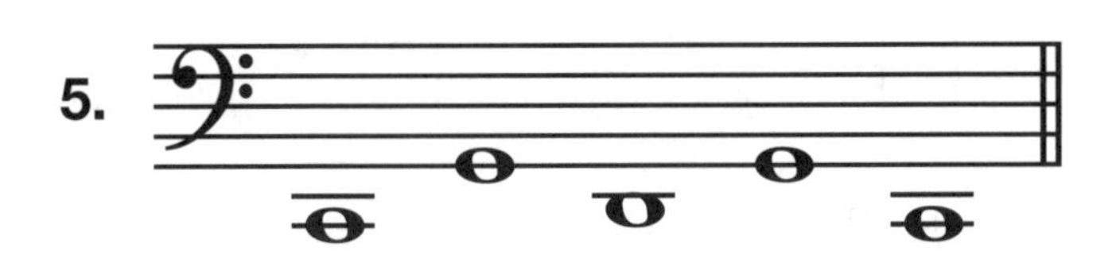

6.

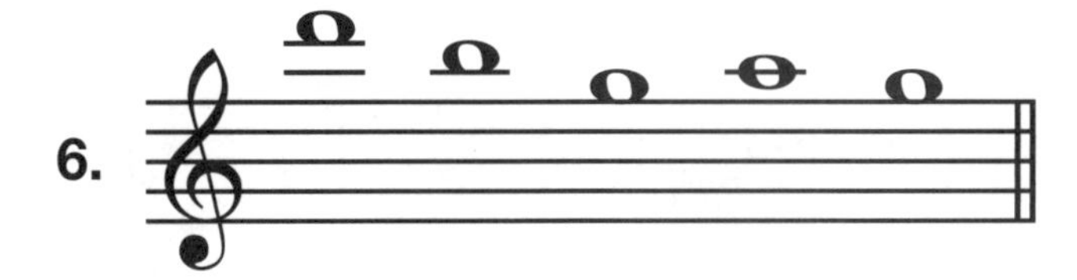

Copying Music

On the upper staff, mark the intervals.
Then play and count the melody, using RH.

On the lower staff:
    Trace the G clef and time signature.
    Copy the melody, one octave lower.

Then play and count what you wrote, using LH.
    Does it sound the same, except an octave lower?

Now play it HT.

Rhythm

Learning about Dotted Quarter Notes

A dotted quarter note fills the time of a quarter note tied to an eighth note.

1. Swing and say the rhyme with a strong rhythmic pulse.

Merrily We Roll Along!

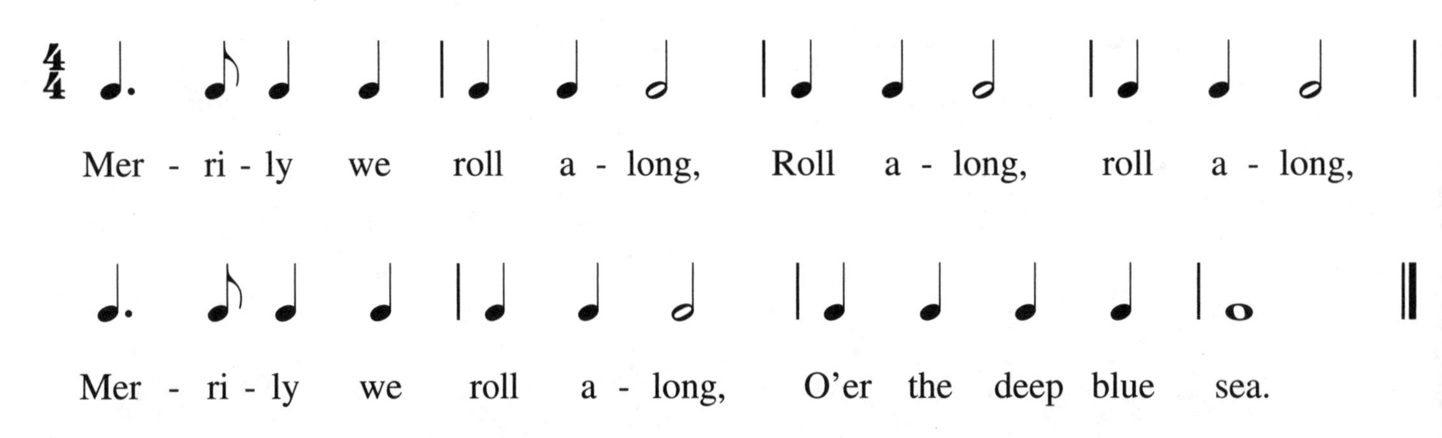

2. Walk the rhythm as you say the rhyme, taking one step for each **pulse**.
3. Walk the rhythm as you say the rhyme again, taking one step for each **note**.

Counting Dotted Quarter Notes

In each of these rhythms, set a strong rhythmic pulse:

1. Point and count.
2. Tap and count.
3. Play and count on any note you choose.

Playing Dotted Quarter Notes

With each of these pieces:

- point and count the rhythm
- tap and count the rhythm
- play and count — RH alone, then LH alone.

Theory

Accompanying and Transposing

To accompany each melody, follow the instructions on page 42.

Merrily We Roll Along uses the notes of the _____ major 5-finger pattern.
TONIC is _____. DOMINANT is _____.

Merrily We Roll Along!

Traditional

Now transpose *Merrily We Roll Along* with your accompaniment to C major.

Sea Chanty uses the notes of the _____ major and minor patterns.
TONIC is _____. DOMINANT is _____.

Sea Chanty

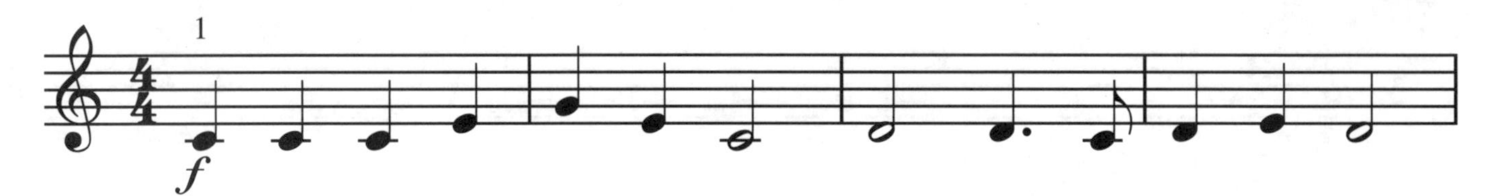

Now transpose *Sea Chanty* with your accompaniment to G major and minor.

Adventures in Sight-Playing

These *Adventures* begin to use 5ths.
Before playing the pieces, practice this exercise until it is smooth and easy.

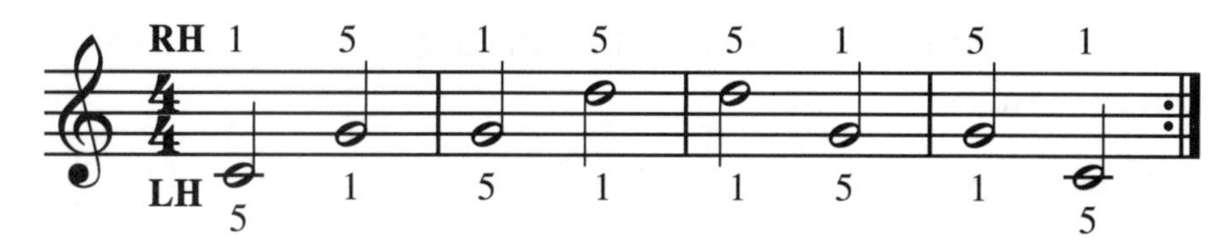

Nothing but 5ths and repeated notes in the next two pieces.

Watch out!
The next two pieces use 4ths and 5ths!
Can you find and circle one 3rd?

Reading

Spot-Placing around High G and Low F

Each of these notes is a Landmark or a 2nd, 3rd, 4th or 5th **above** or **below** a Landmark.

Spot-place each note and write its name on the line.

Playing Intervals around High G and Low F

Mark the intervals.
Spot-place the first note.
Then play and say the direction, intervals, and note names.

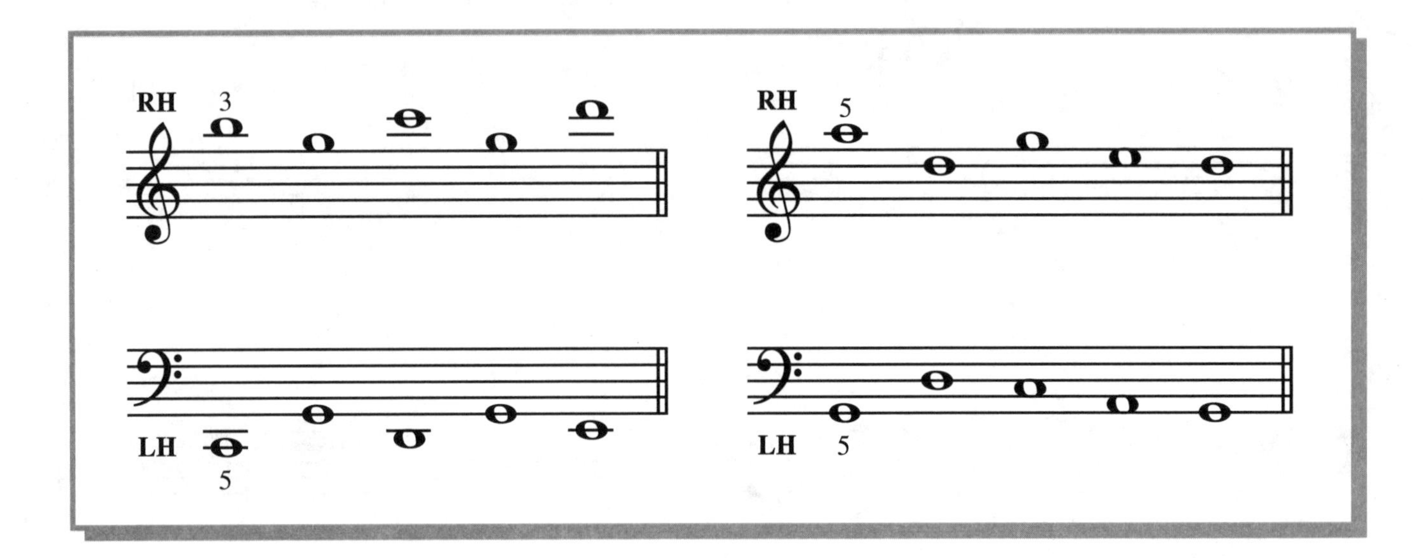

For correlated Discoveries, Repertoire and Technic, see MUSIC TREE 2A, pages 54-58.

Copying Music

On the lower staff, mark the intervals.
Then play and count the melody, using LH.

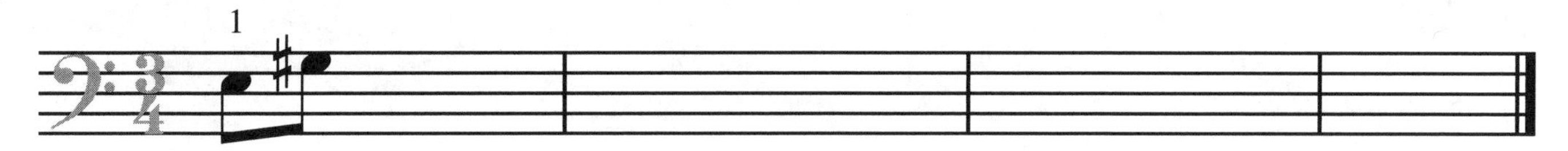

On the upper staff:
  Trace the F clef and time signature.
  Copy the melody, one octave higher.

Then play and count what you wrote, using RH.
  Does it sound the same, except an octave higher?

Now play it HT.

Theory

Accompanying and Transposing

To accompany this melody, follow the instructions on page 42.
Polish Song uses the notes of the _____ major 5-finger pattern.
Tonic is _____. Dominant is _____.

Polish Song

Now transpose *Polish Song* with your accompaniment to F major.

Walking Dotted Quarter Notes

1. Swing and say the rhyme with a strong rhythmic pulse.

America

3/4

My coun - try 'tis of thee,

Sweet land of lib - er - ty

Of thee I sing;

Land where my fa - thers died,

Land of the pil - grims' pride,

From eve - ry__ moun - tain-side

Let__ free - dom ring.

2. Walk the rhythm as you say the rhyme, taking one step for each **pulse**.
3. Walk the rhythm as you say the rhyme again, taking one step for each **note**.

Counting Dotted Quarter Notes

In each of these rhythms, set a strong rhythmic pulse:

1. Point and count.
2. Tap and count.
3. Play and count on any note you choose.

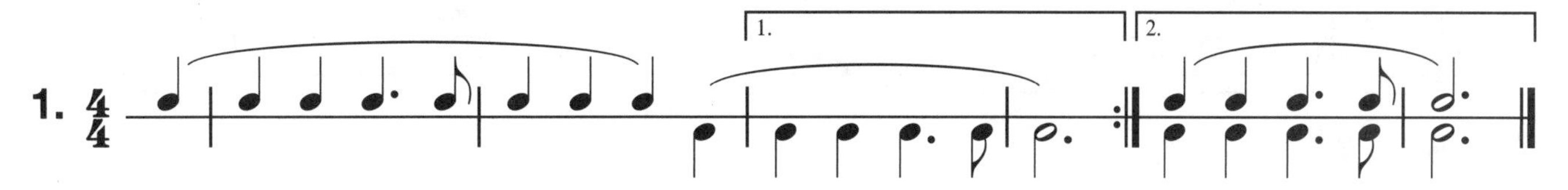

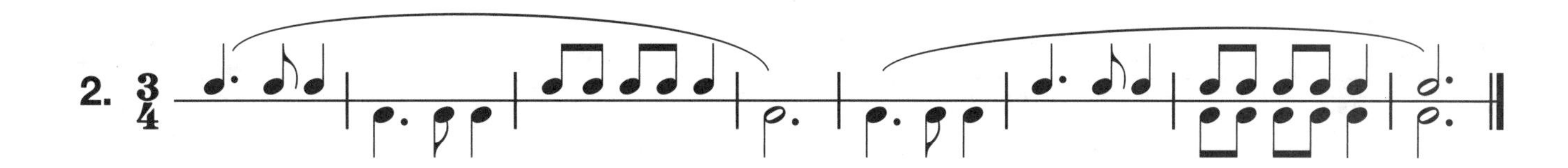

Matching

Draw a line to connect the boxes that have the same number of pulses.

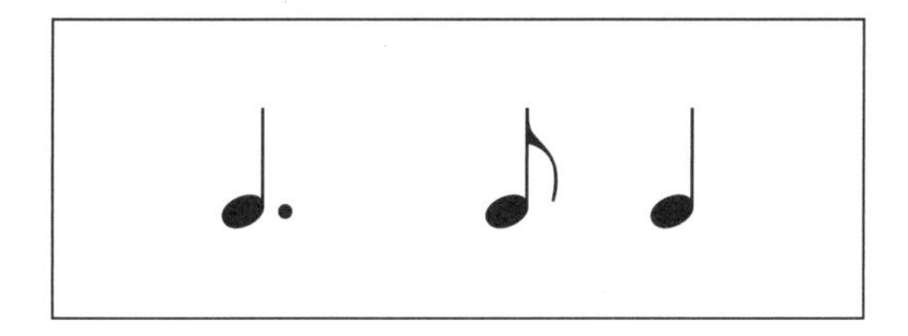

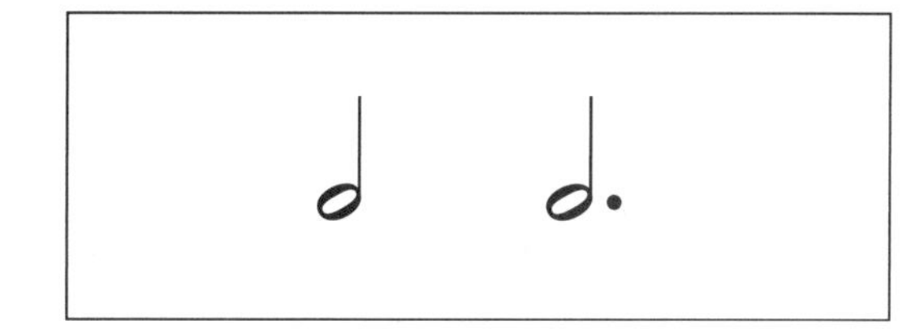

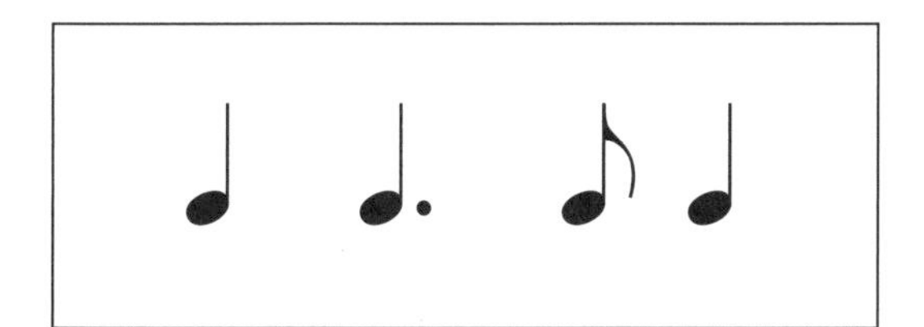

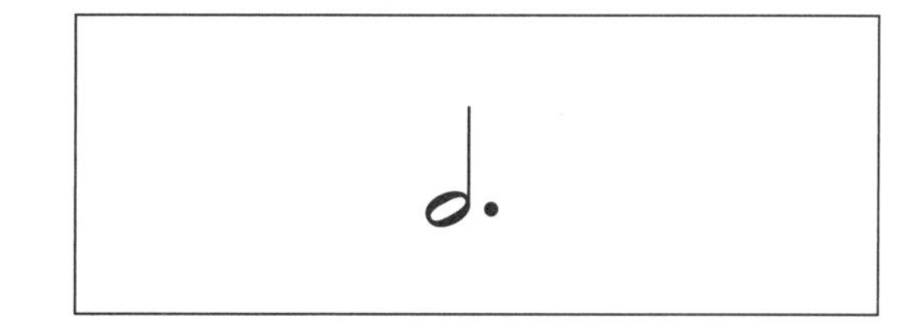

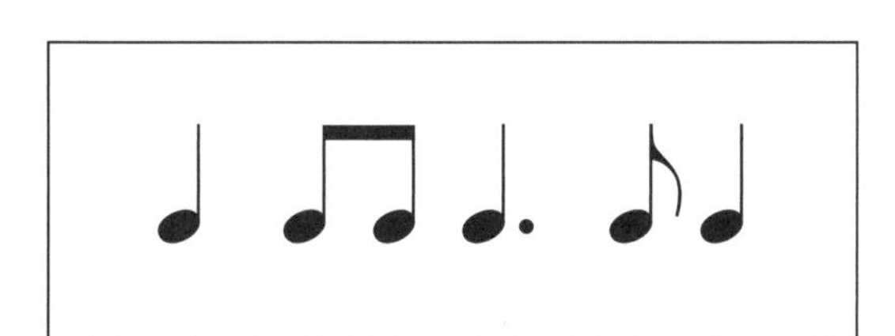

Sight-Playing

Each of these pieces begins on one of your new Landmarks!

Nos. 1 and 2 go up from Landmark ____________________.

Nos. 3 and 4 go down from Landmark __________________.

Crossword Puzzle

Draw a line to connect each sign with its name.

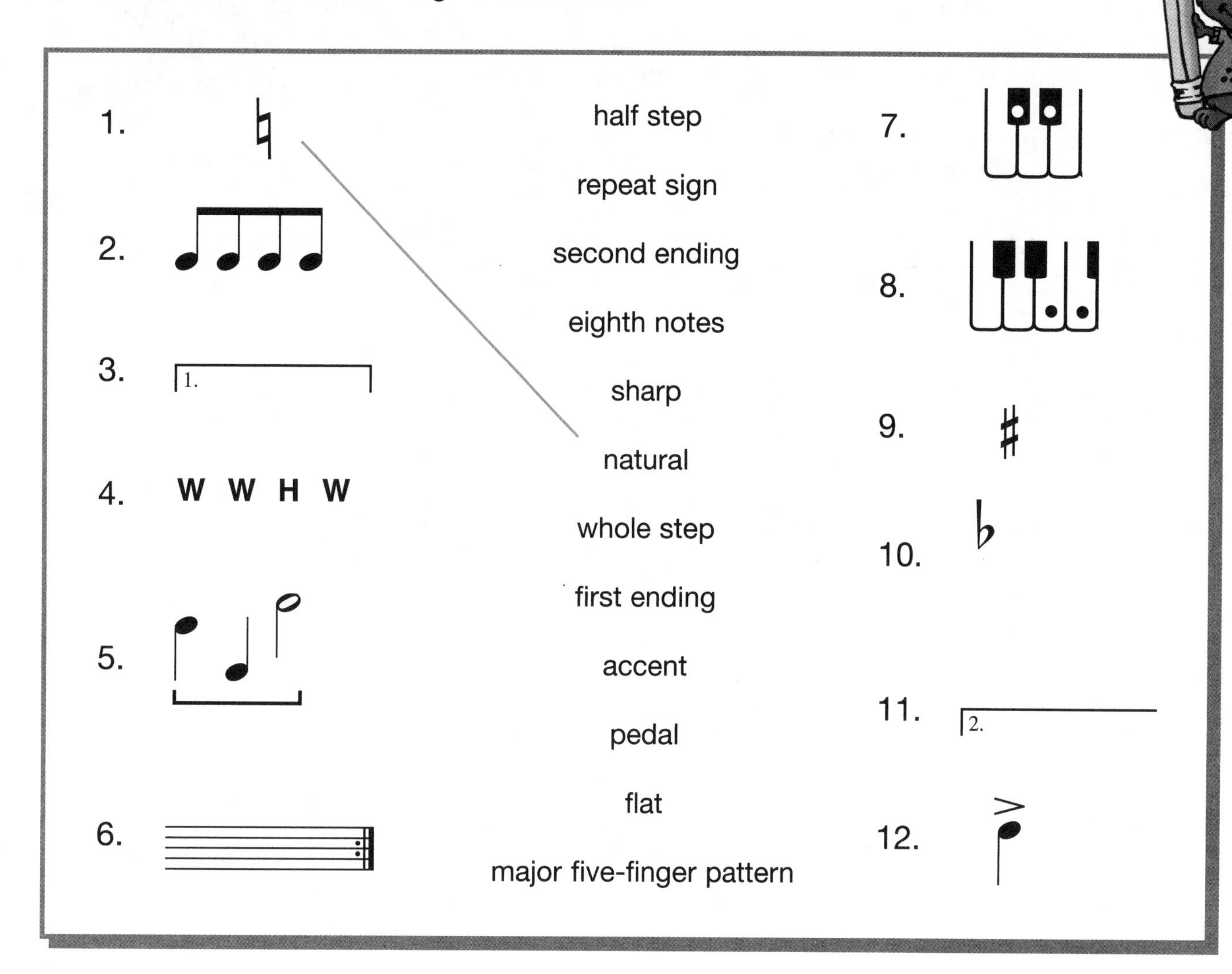

Check your work! Write the name for each sign in this crossword puzzle.

Reading

Naming Notes

Circle the correct music for each group of letter names.

For correlated Discoveries, Repertoire and Technic, see MUSIC TREE 2A, pages 59-64.

Playing Intervals around High G and Low F

Mark the intervals.
Spot-place the first note.
Then play and say the direction, intervals, and note names.
Each hand begins on thumb or 5th finger.

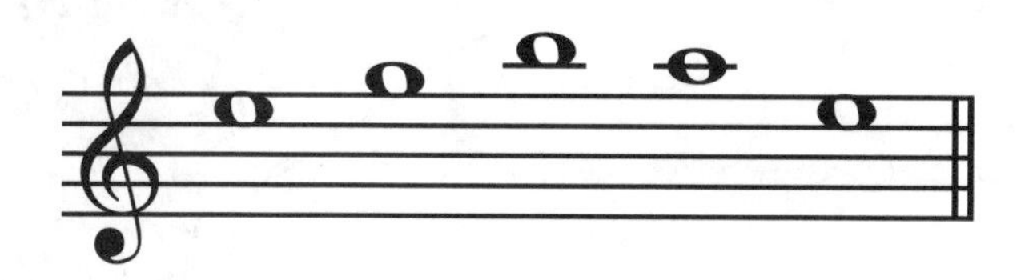

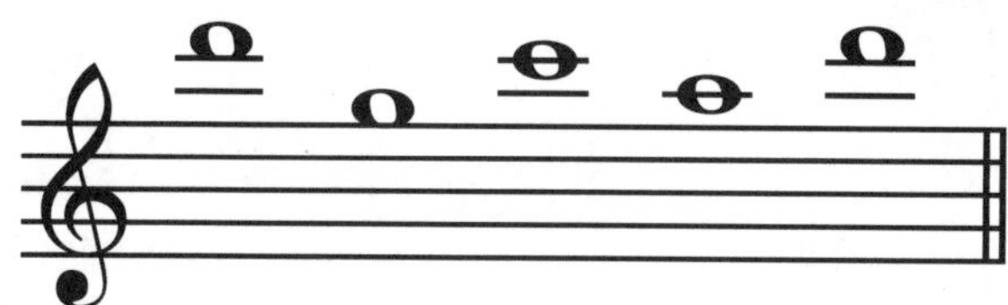

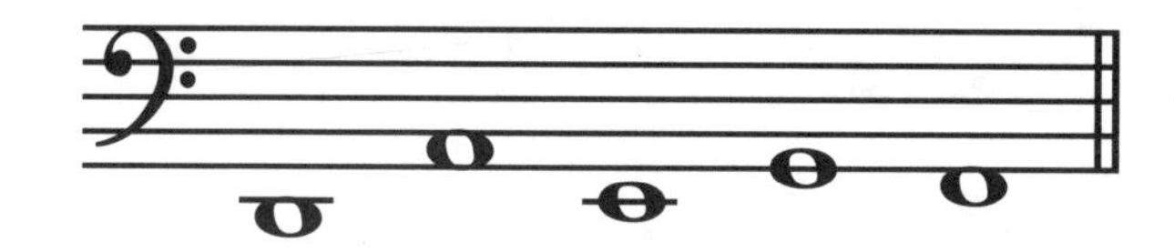

Copying Music

On the upper staff, mark the intervals.
Then play and count the melody, using RH.

On the lower staff:

Trace the G clef and time signature.
Copy the melody, one octave lower.

Then play and count what you wrote, using LH.

Does it sound the same, except an octave lower?

Now play HT.

Rhythm

Eighth Rests 𝄾

An eighth rest is a sign for silence as long as an eighth note.

1. Swing and say the rhyme with a strong rhythmic pulse.

Beginning Typist

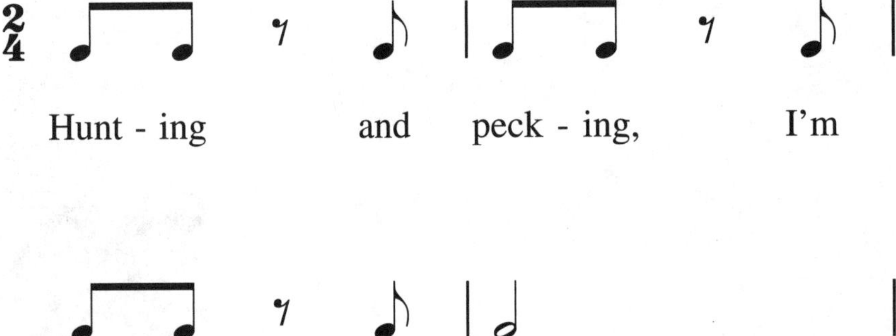

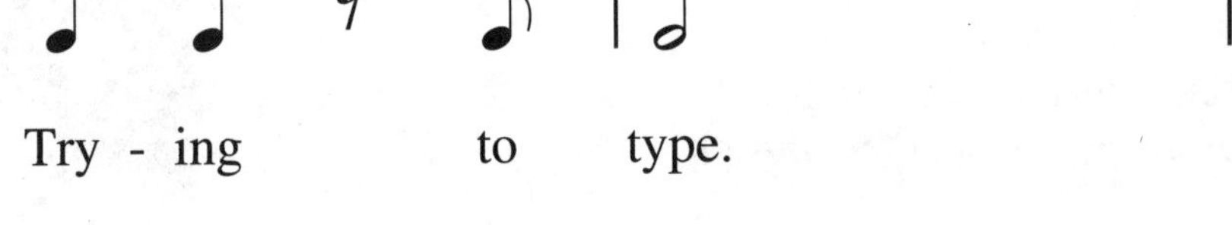

2. Walk the rhythm as you say the rhyme, taking one step for each **pulse**.
3. Walk the rhythm as you say the rhyme again, taking one step for each **note**.

Counting Eighth Rests

In each of these rhythms, set a strong rhythmic pulse:

1. Point and count.
2. Tap and count.
3. Play and count — LH on G♯, RH on D♯.

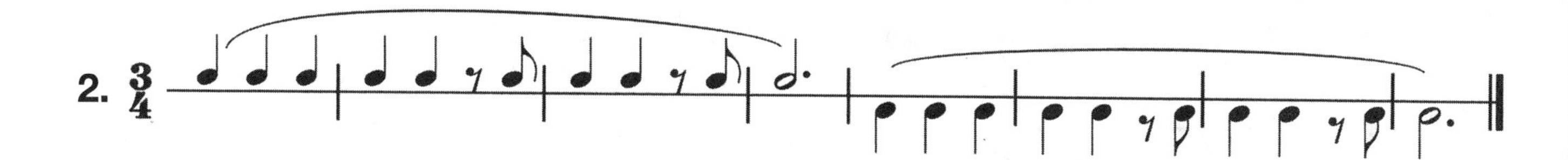

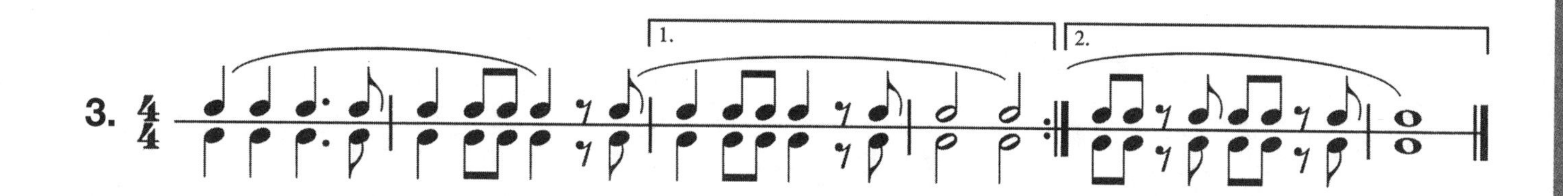

Playing Eighth Rests

With each of these pieces:

- point and count the rhythm.
- tap and count the rhythm.
- play and count — RH alone, then LH alone.

Theory

Accompanying and Transposing

To accompany each melody, follow the instructions on page 42.

Goin' Home uses the notes of the _____ major five-finger pattern.
TONIC is _____. DOMINANT is _____.

Goin' Home

Now transpose *Goin' Home* with your accompaniment to D major.

Gypsy Dance uses the notes of the _____ minor five-finger pattern.
TONIC is _____. DOMINANT is _____.

Gypsy Dance

Now transpose *Gypsy Dance* with your accompaniment to D minor.

Sight-Playing

These pieces have some tricky rhythms!

A slow, steady tempo and a full tone will help you play accurately the first time.

Watch out for dotted quarter and eighth notes.

Watch out for the eighth rests.

Get ready for a big move!

Glossary

two eighth notes	♫	Fill the time of one quarter note
one eighth note	♪	Fills half the time of one quarter note
dotted quarter note	♩.	Fills the time of a quarter note tied to an eighth note
eighth rest	𝄾	Sign for silence as long as an eighth note
damper pedal		Hold damper pedal down
first and second endings	1. 2.	Play through the **first** ending, repeat, then skip the first ending and play the **second** ending instead
a tempo		Italian for "go on in time"
accent	>	Play with extra stress
dominant	V	The fifth degree of any five-finger pattern
fortissimo	*ff*	Italian for "very loud"
fermata	𝄐	Pause
half step		From one key to the very next key
Low F		The F below Bass F
High G		The G above Treble G
major five-finger pattern		A pattern of five tones made entirely of whole steps except for a half step between degrees 3 and 4
major triad		Degrees 1, 3, and 5 of any major five-finger pattern
minor five-finger pattern		A pattern of five tones made entirely of whole steps except for a half step between degrees 2 and 3
minor triad		Degrees 1, 3, and 5 of any minor five-finger pattern
pianissimo	*pp*	Italian for "very soft"
ritardando	*rit.*	Italian for "gradually slower"
tonic	I	The first degree of any five-finger pattern
whole step		A whole step is made of two half steps with one key skipped